The LOVEBYRDS' STORY

How the Class Clown and the Class President Developed an Extraordinary Love

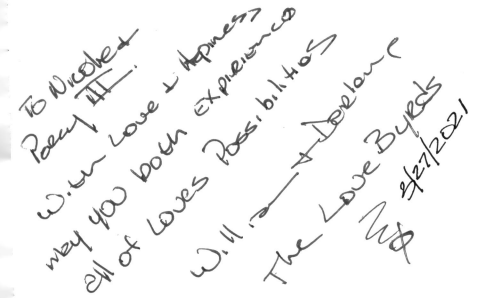

To Nicohed Perry III.
W/the Love & Happiness
may you both experience
all of Loves Possibilities
W. ll. — Deretone
The Love Byrds
8/27/2021
MB

The LOVEBYRDS' STORY

HOW THE CLASS CLOWN AND THE CLASS PRESIDENT DEVELOPED AN EXTRAORDINARY LOVE

WILLIAM BYRD & DARLENE BYRD

Love-Byrds

Atlanta, Georgia

Connect with the Love-Byrds

Download your bonus worksheets and learn
more about our work with couples at

Love-Byrds.com/paperbookbonusfiles

FOREWORD

Pastor Gregory Washington,
Author and Spiritual Advisor

*T*here are times in the History of the Kingdom of God and the Body of Christ, where God raises up young leaders; leaders whom God recognizes as His Bride and Remnant. A lot of what is being displayed in the Body of Christ today God does not recognize as His own.

William & Darlene Byrd not only have Christ in them but also the Hope of Glory. God recognizes them, he has appointed them and anointed them for this *kairos* (opportune time) moment in the history of the Kingdom of God and in these absolutely crazy times we find ourselves in.

I met William several years ago in Must Ministries Homeless Shelter. He came broken, but with a plan. His plan, "I want to break free from life-controlling issues/substances, obtain employment, renew my craft, obtain housing, and renew my relationship with God." The roller coaster wasn't an easy ride, of course, but who said it would ever be. While in the shelter, he inspired others with his "navy-veteran" discipline and organizational skills, which were much needed in a world of chaos. So now, years later William has found his match, truly made in heaven, a phenomenal woman and Prophet of God. She helps to make him whole. God is birthing a Marriage Enrichment Ministry in this awesome couple, and rightfully so. They look so much like the Bride of Christ and they represent the Bride of Christ.

These moments in History are rare, and THE FATHER OF LIGHTS KNOWS EXACTLY WHAT HE'S DOING.

CHAPTERS OF LOVE

MEET THE BYRDS

~Welcome to Our Love Story ~

"**Y**ou did not choose me, but I chose you and appointed you so that you might go and bear lasting fruit – so that whatever you ask in my name, the Father will give to you." (John 15:16) We all have hopes and dreams that we would one day achieve something so great, it would be beyond our wildest imaginations. As for us, we always knew that we were given a special call – a call to love. We proudly earned the call of the Love Byrds. Every journey begins with a choice. A single step in the right direction can propel you into the highest levels of an empowered life. One of the main purposes of our love journey is to encourage others that true love is possible. It is our desire that our love story would help to uncover the hidden treasures within us and enhance relationships along the way.

Our journey of love began long before either of us realized that we were being groomed for one another. We've experienced many pivotal points prior to being brought together, to make this dream a reality. We knew we needed an extraordinary love to withstand past relationship experiences, everyday bad choices and our past hurts. From the very beginning, our relationship was predisposed to twists and turns, unthinkable for most couples. Suffice it to say, growing up, we've traveled very different paths, but in the end, two paths collided, and our destiny ensued. Our individual dreams created and called into existence what we specifically wanted in a mate (without ever knowing that we would truly one day find it.) Yet, we were brought together, as one, for a purpose.

We focused on the possibility that God could bring the most unlikely couple together for one sole purpose – to serve and love one another selflessly. "God has chosen the foolish things of the world to confound the wise; and God has chosen the weak things of the world to confound the things which are mighty." (1 Corinthians 1:27) We are called lovers of love. God is love–and we seek *this* kind of love through our passion to please one another. This is no ordinary love, but we know the love that brought us together is the love we found in one another through our love for Jesus Christ and the answered prayers of our elders.

Love is an action word. One of our guiding principles for action: "Do nothing out of selfish ambition or vain conceit. Rather, in humility value others above yourselves, not looking to your own interests but each of you to the interests of the other." (Philippians 2:3-4) Today, we believe acting on our values is truly a foundational part of our love story. We focus on words like serving, loving, honesty, dedication, commitment, consistency, steadiness, and diligence; to name a few. These values create an environment that consistently draws out the best of each of us. We allow nothing to come between our love for each other nor our love for our God. (Jeremiah 31:3)

As we share our love story, we hope that from our experiences you can gain positive takeaways to use in your own life and relationship. Strong relationships require work, effort, and intentionality, on both parts. We pray that the message you receive, demonstrated in our core values and guiding principles, assist you in strengthening your relationships and/or marital bond. The set of core values, which you will see threaded throughout our stories, are intended to not only show how we consistently challenge to out-serve one another but also to highlight the grace of God on our marriage.

In His service,
Billy & Darlene Byrd

The Class Clown and the Class President

HIM

*Your Past Should Not
Control Your Future*

My parents were young, high school lovers who were married straight out of high school. Planning for a family was not first and foremost in the minds of two young lovers. My parents had plans like every other high school graduate. Yet unexpectedly, in 1964 I was born and then my brother and sister were born shortly thereafter. Life was wonderful for the young lovers. They were ecstatic with the new additions to the family. My father, who always dreamed of a first-born son, could not have asked for a more suitable blessing.

We were a loving, close-knit family. My mom was super supportive of my dad's dreams and aspirations. She also had dreams of her own. Raising her children to be strong spiritually and academically, with great character, was a top priority. My father was the consummate disciplinarian, provider, and protector. He owned an upholstery business, which is where I noticed his ability to bring life to hopeless furniture.

The entire Byrd family was well-known in our small hometown in Pennsylvania. My father always wanted to raise his first-born son as a warrior, to be a mirror image of his strength, drive, passion, and especially his love for family. I witnessed his work ethic first-hand. I admired his masterful, hard work and I promised that I would emulate it to the fullest. In my high school years, my father taught me everything I knew about reupholstering. I learned a lot through his guidance and expertise. To no one's surprise, I became exceptional at reupholstering furniture. I could fix or upholster just about anything. My father's wish for a son to take on his mirror image was suddenly beginning to take shape.

My strong academic background was a result of years of private school education. Daily exposure to moral role models was significant in my upbringing. I had a solid religious and educational foundation, and all had a huge impact on my development spiritually, educationally, and emotionally. I was surrounded by students in school, all growing in the same direction. This experience was one part of the bedrock of my focus on good character. I excelled in many areas of my life due to the rigorous teaching in parochial school.

The transition from private school to public school in my junior year of high school was an incredible story in and of itself. When I enrolled in public school, my private school education placed me a year ahead. Getting good grades was not difficult at all. I would complete my work at school and have plenty of time to do things that I liked. I had plenty of time to clown around in class. I became the popular student affectionately known as *The Class Clown*. The class clown was a way of adapting to all the changes that suddenly took place around me in my junior and senior year of high school. The course of my life took a drastic turn. Certain situations occurred during my early upbringing that put me in a place of having to fend for my life on my own. These situations were mostly brought on by the unexpected turn of events that took place involving my dad. You have this strong, domineering man, who leads his family with love, protection, and strength, suddenly becomes completely succumbed to and overtaken by the use of drugs and substances. It affected his relationship with the very people he loved. Clowning around and bringing laughter to myself and others made life more bearable.

HER

Your Past Predicts Your Future

hey say natural leaders are born. I say born leaders are rare. You can tell a true leader by how they take charge without even thinking about it. They typically do not wait to be told what to do. They come up with the idea, map it out, and then effortlessly lead the charge. You will know you're dealing with a leader when you find yourself being completely engulfed with making their ideas a reality. A true leader is proactive, inspiring, encouraging, and supportive. While growing up, I would hear people say, "She is no average, ordinary girl...Darlene is a born leader." I never really understood what they meant, nor why was it so evident to everyone except for me. I was just being me. Being me, just came naturally. While I never focused on being a leader, I always knew I was comfortable taking charge and leading without being asked. In high school, I was well-known for my leadership qualities, and my wide, warm embrace of people.

My propensity for high academic achievements afforded me opportunities to lead and encourage others to follow. From my perspective, I was just being me. Unforced.

While the primary focus, for most young girls my age, would be attending parties, going to the movies, and going to the mall, I made no pretenses that my academics, working, and caring for my younger siblings were my main priorities. I looked after and protected my siblings. One sister was less than a year younger and my baby sister was three years younger. I also had a brother who was several years younger. When it came to love, protection, and nurture, they knew I was a reliable person they could count on.

True signs of adulthood are maturity and responsibility; characteristics I quickly developed in my family, and it kept us grounded. In this situation, being the older sister and having to supervise younger siblings posed no negative animosity. Instead, it made us extremely close and afforded us opportunities to learn self-confidence and how to take responsibility.

Focusing on my studies, working, and caring for siblings left me very little time for fun and games. At times, I would participate in school sports and activities with a group of close, like-minded, sister-friends. Field hockey was my favorite. I focused mostly on what I perceived to be my worldview—how I could fit perfectly in the field of business in America.

My leadership qualities came to light while growing up with my siblings. Caring for them taught me how to be strong, even in the times I may have felt overwhelmed. It heightened my sense of self-awareness. I learned that I was motivated by my ability to love and care for others. I skipped right through the fallacy of the blustering teen-adolescent years. My teen years seemed to have passed me by, but I didn't feel I was missing out on much of anything. Besides, I had my hands full, doing what had to be done for my siblings and the upkeep of my family.

Caring for my family and achieving new and exciting accomplishments have always been a source of pride. I love setting goals and reaching them. My determination for achieving success was prompted by my desire for the opportunity, to one day take responsibility and financially care for my own family. I was known for many great things while in high school but upon graduating with the class of 1983, the fondest achievement was being called *The Class President*.

REFLECTIONS

What strategies have you employed to make life more bearable?

What qualities did you demonstrate in your youth that fully developed as an adult?

THE BROKEN ROAD:
LOST LOVE

HIM

When the Winds and Waves
Crush Your Dreams

*T*here is a war raging in the hearts of every man. The war is internal and there is only one casualty – one's self. The heart makes you feel one thing, but the mind tells you something totally different. I am a true example of this notion. I have always had a strong will. I have never been accused of being easily swayed by the opinions of others. Once I set my mind to doing something, it is safe to say I will get it done. Even though at times, I have been known to settle for the less desirable in the area of relationships, I knew it would only be temporary. I have learned you never have to accept words spoken of you that do not line up with how you see yourself. No matter what, I always believed that I would serve a special mission in my life. I longed to find and love a special woman who was deserving of my love. That search has taken me through many twists and turns, up until the moment I laid eyes on Darlene. My search may not have always looked pretty, but it certainly was always motivated by good intentions.

Much of who we are today is a product of our past. The good news is that we do not have to be held prisoners to any negative impact we may have experienced. Each of our relationships plays a part in who we become. Family life is important because it provides unconditional love, support, and a sense of belonging. It also creates a framework of our value for others. When this is present in your family, it will significantly shape the quality of your character. And when we take the time to evaluate our past, it gives us insight into how our lives have been shaped, based on what we have learned.

The roads of life often lead to many unexpected turns. The lessons we learn from our life journey could be valuable, amazing, and thought-provoking. There is no truer quote than the one that speaks of how *"difficult roads often lead to beautiful destinations."* When you have strong beliefs, the destination makes the journey worthwhile. The fires of life are not to **resign** you, but they are to **refine** you into the person you were designed to be.

My Grandmother was very instrumental in our spiritual growth and development. She taught us how to be overall good people. We learned good character traits by watching how our grandmother lived her life. She was a dedicated member of Shiloh Baptist Church.

We spent a lot of time with her doing her church duties. She was our introduction to deep religious beliefs. She always taught us that no one chooses the devil, but he can choose you so always be watchful and pray in every situation. The Baptist teaching was big on loving one another. It is where I learned about living a life that is pleasing to the Lord. My grandmother lived in The Bennett Homes Project. I was exposed to and got along with people from all walks of life.

In 1971, when I was ten years old, we were displaced by a devastating flood in the city of Chester, Pa. Between 1971 and 1972, our family was in transition. After being displaced, we moved into a beautiful home in Sharon Hill. It was amazing to be living in Sharon Hill. My parents were able to buy a new home from the home insurance payout. They were brand spanking new homes. Shortly following the move to Sharon Hill, my mother and fathers' first breakup occurred. Mom decided to relocate us to Savannah, Georgia for two years. We really loved Savannah. We were in Savannah during the bicentennial celebrations. My mom took us to see the Freedom Train in Savannah. We had a blast. It felt like a long vacation. But then suddenly mom decided she would take us back home to rejoin with dad. Things were not much different from when we left. It wasn't long after being home that we were taking off again. This time mom took our family and we headed north to Massachusetts. We lived in Massachusetts for about a year and a half before once again returning home to rejoin with dad.

One evening while my mom was at work, my father went into a weird psychotic episode. He started hallucinating and tripping. This was a total shock for all of us to witness. Looking back at it now from what I know, I believe it was an acid trip. I have seen people on an acid trip before. I remember it got so bad he started breaking our furniture in the house. He completely shattered the dining room table and chairs. He took the chairs and started crashing them on the table. My sister was just a baby. I grabbed her and my brother and took them to one of our neighbors' houses. I explained that something was seriously wrong with my dad. The paramedics were called but by the time they arrived I was long gone. When I came back home that night, I remember coming in the house and as I was on my way up the stairs, I overheard my mom talking to dad in the living room. I heard him asking mom "Did the kids see me like that?" That gave me a lot of insight. I did not know then, but I never forgot about that exchange. The evidence was my father was tripping. He could not recall we were all in the house witnessing all the furniture being completely shattered. He was never the same after that. Things at home became progressively worse. It went the other way on a downward spiral. We went from living in a beautiful home and having a loving family to total dysfunction. My brother and I once wore tailor-made clothes, suits, and ties every day and attended Catholic school. Now, our father was doing the unthinkable as our family laid in ruins. We could have never imagined seeing our father take such a drastic downturn in his life. It was as if he was giving up on us and his own life.

The loving part about my father is that up until this point, we were a very happy, stable family. We grew up going on family vacations to Great Adventure amusement park every summer and had great family get-aways. We were showered with love and affection from my father. As things were all beginning to change, my father grew agitated and angry. He became very abusive toward all of us, including my mom. Alcohol definitely played a major part in my father's change of attitude toward caring for his family.

I remember one year, we all got bikes for Christmas. It snowed for weeks after Christmas and we were getting anxious to ride our bikes. I had a green chopper bike with big handlebars decorated with streamers. I did not get a chance to ride my bike all winter long. When the snow let up and it was finally warm enough to go outside, I could not wait to take a ride up the hill and all through the neighborhood. As I was on my way back, I could see that the garage door was ajar. I pulled in the driveway and there was my father standing with one arm behind his back and one swinging a stick. He slowly turned toward me to walk out of the garage into the street. I was pulling up on the right side of the yard. Next thing I knew I was off the bike and on the ground staring up at the sky. He just started beating me repeatedly. I saw the anger in his eyes unlike I have ever seen before. I was in big trouble. This is the kicker. As he was hitting me, he did not say a word. Without showing any emotions at all, he just walked back into the house almost like a zombie. He beat me up pretty badly. That changed my whole perspective of my father. From that point on, I was fearful of my father. I was afraid he could unintentionally kill me by the way he was beating me.

Typically, my mom would be the only one in the house to escape my dad's wrath when he became agitated. But then he started beating my mother over the slightest of situations. My mother was getting beaten like crazy. Still, she would not let anyone talk ill about dad. In my opinion, she was a committed wife to a fault. Despite everything my dad put her and her children through she remained committed to her marriage. I never understood it. Even though my mother had the courage to leave my father several times, I could tell by the sadness in her eyes that she would always return. I was starting to hate being in the house. No matter how hard we tried to keep the peace in the house, he would fly off the handle for any or no reason at all. I would do all the things he wanted me to do. I learned how to handle his business so well that I could operate it without him being in the shop. Nothing I did to stay in his good graces saved me from his constant, savage beatings. The final break for me was when he began beating me and we got into a serious fistfight. It was the point of no return. As a result, I became a complete rebel. That was the day I left the house and I never returned to live in my father's house ever again. My mom would send people to try to find me to tell me to come home. She knew when I was done, I would never return.

I was staying with my friend, Chris, whose stepmom had recently passed. I stayed with him all summer. I spent half my time at Chris and Pooch's house. We were all best friends and looked out for each other. We would hang out every night all summer long before I left to go into the Navy. When we graduated from school, I would stay out all night in the streets. I just kept going all day until late into the night. When I finally made it back to my friend's house, I would go directly to bed. I made sure I was so tired that going straight to sleep would be easy. I did not want to think about anything going on at home.

Growing up, I was popular and traveled in many different circles. You could always count on seeing me at every sporting event and every school party. There was not much fun I would miss out on. If it was happening, I was there in the mix. I was usually the loud one and the life of the party. The qualities that I demonstrated growing up, shaped me and helped me get through various hard, life transitions. Looking back at my high school days, I remember when my good friends and I created a group of A-track students. The group's purpose was to demonstrate academic excellence while still maintaining our coolness and popularity at the same time. United Fly Guys (UFG) was a self-initiated college preparatory group of well-dressed male students who strived for academic excellence. Today, I am not much different from that guy who loved to love, have fun, and who loved to look cool doing so in the hopes that I could provoke some to aim for greatness.

Like most youth from my small town, transitioning through the basic stages of life was challenging. For me, life seemed serious but normal most of my life until tragedy hit. My family life unexpectedly became completely chaotic. It started with the flood that cost my family the comfort of our beautiful home in 1971. The stability that kept the family close began to unravel. My parents later divorced under the pressures of emotional turmoil. Of course, this took an unbearable impact on everything I viewed as worthwhile in life.

After our house flooded and after my parents' divorce, these were not ideal times for us as a family. These life-changing events shook me to my core. It was extremely difficult for me to handle the sadness because I was always the happy-go-lucky kind of guy. So, I created a persona to joke my way through the pain I was experiencing watching the safety of my family life change so drastically. By 1982, when most students were preparing for senior year activities and graduation, I had a secret that I could tell no one; not even my parents.

All through the years, I was working in my father's shop. In my mind, a lot of that was forced labor. I did not like it then, but I am grateful for the experience today. It was the most intriguing and fulfilling thing I was doing. It brought me promising opportunities in the community. I would pull up to people's homes with their sofa in my dad's van. It was a fascinating feeling. When the kids in the neighborhood would see me and my brother bringing their sofa into the house, they would look at us in awe because we were so young. Working with dad in the shop came with pain and perks. I was driving my dad's car and van at a young age delivering furniture. No young people were doing what I was doing at this point. I would come straight to the shop after school to help with things around the shop, finish out the books, and lock up the shop. They were building blocks and there were some perks from that as well. There was a work ethic I gained from that. I learned a lot of resiliency and I learned how to be tough as nails. I learned how to not let anything really bother me. I became the most capable person I ever thought I could be. I could deal with a lot of things. I was knowledgeable about a lot of stuff. I would drive people crazy with how much I knew about different topics. The class clown was a way of adapting to the harsh reality that my family was failing.

During this runaway period, to escape life as it were, I signed up for a Delayed Entry Program, which allowed me to enlist in the Navy upon graduation, without parental consent. I did not tell my mom or dad. My family did not know anything about my decision. One day, I scheduled a meeting with the Navy recruiter. I purposely scheduled a meeting at our house at a time that I assumed my dad would still be at work. My mom answered the door and said, "There is a gentleman here from the Navy to see you, Billy." My dad was home sitting in the living room. They had no idea who the tall distinguished gentleman was asking to see me. I had already made my final decision to go to the Navy instead of attending college. There was no changing my mind. At that point, I really did not care what either of them thought about my decision. I was doing what I thought was best for me. In my mind, I had no family. It was time I looked out for myself. I was out on my own. I would go home occasionally to get clothes but by the time the summer was over, I was scheduled to depart for boot camp in early fall. My parents could not find me all summer, and I did not reach out to them at all. Although, I would see my brother at the basketball courts or hanging out with our old friends. I would see my mother and sister on their Sunday visits to my grandmother's house. Other than that, I was nowhere to be found. You were not finding me anywhere in Chester unless I wanted to be found. I was running around the city without a care in the world. Sometimes I would play basketball on the Eastside until the break of dawn. I was up all times of the night in the Fairgrounds, on street corners; I was everywhere. The dynamics of our family relationship had changed drastically after my decision to go into the Navy, which also probably negatively affected my life.

A combination of major life-changing events forced me to quickly grow into an independent, responsible adult. Discipline has always been a character trait, but while I was in the Navy it really began to take shape. These were defining moments that would set the course of my entire life. They were also turning points. After a brief time away, I returned home and things were different from when I left. Although my father was still residing at home, my mother and sisters had moved into a new place of their own. My brother had enlisted in the Army, and the family unit was completely separated.

After a few years, my father was diagnosed with cancer. He sold the family house and moved his shop into a two-story building. He used the first floor for his shop, and he lived on the top floor of that building. At some point, he became too ill to care for himself, so my mom moved back in with him as his caregiver.

My father was so headstrong I thought he would beat cancer as he did every other battle. As a Muslim, he had a strong commitment to his faith. The cancer began taking a toll on his body. He felt strongly that he would beat it. I believed him. He was going through chemo and it was eating him away. He was fighting as hard as he could. The sickness was brutally attacking his body and suddenly I started losing hope. He had been given six months to live after the initial surgery, but he lived another year and seven months.

While dad was extremely ill, my parents renewed their wedding vows once again just before dad passed away. I remember going over to visit dad. He was bedridden with pain so severe he did not realize I was there talking to him. He started saying something under his breath but I could not make out what he was saying. At one point, it sounded like he was trying to apologize for how he had treated my mom. He always said it was important to him that my mom receives all his pension should anything happen to him.

The thought of losing my dad was unbearable. Losing someone you love can wreak havoc on your mental and physical life. At the same time, my family was dealing with my dad's sickness, I was having my issues to deal with. Although my father was not in agreement, I married a friend of mine at a young age. I spent so much time trying to prove to him and others that my decision to marry was sound and it would work out best for both of us. I was desperately trying to win over my dad to prove to him that I made a mature decision. Although I prayed that I would one day win his favor and he would eventually approve of the marriage, he never hid his strong feelings regarding that marriage. He was not necessarily against me getting married so young, but he was vehemently against the person whom I chose to be my wife. He did not think she was the person for me. He tried to convince me that I could find someone whom I could love and not be required to care for someone else's six children. He wanted me to find someone who would be worthy of my love according to how I was raised to love and care for family. At the time, I did not agree with his ideas because I felt like I was demonstrating love in my family even though the children were not mine. What people know about me is that I am always happy and full of laughter. I seek peace in every situation, so the more my father tried to convince me against what I felt was right, the more determined I was to make the marriage situation work.

After years of serving and giving, I was beginning to feel burned out. While I felt it was my duty to love my wife and her children equally, the relationship was completely imbalanced. The more I gave, the more I was being taken advantage of. I never felt like my love was appreciated. As long as I continued to do everything for everybody, there were no complaints. Therefore, something was seriously missing in my own family. After years of various substantial issues in an unfulfilled marriage, we both agreed the marriage should end. It was a tough decision to make because there were children involved. Children are a gift from God. I love my children with a deep love. I would do anything to ensure their safety and well-being. I realized, no matter what, I could continue to provide for my children and be there for them whenever they needed me. One main characteristic I learned from my father is to have genuine love for your family. He taught me his strong belief in being the kind of provider for our family as our heavenly Father provides for us.

As things began to unfold, I found myself feeling lost and lonely. All I wanted was to be loved and to love someone worthy of my love. Losing love can be both a physical and mental loss. My first lost love was a physical loss with the loss of my dad in 1996. We were devastated, losing the leader and warrior of our family. The mental loss that I experienced was the idea of being denied the true love I had always hoped for, as well as the vision and passion I had longed for in my life. I once desired to be loved so deeply that it created perfect opportunities for being taken advantage of. I needed a break. Thus, my downward spiral began.

Unfortunately, after the marriage ended, I found myself looking for love in all the wrong places. This set me on a path of jumping in and out of relationships looking for the perfect one to share my true love and affection with. My past relationships were my greatest disappointments. I found myself in and out of bad relationships with different women looking for love, but finding unequal, imbalanced relationships that were unhealthy for all involved. This need for love stemmed from my background growing up. I have since learned that adequately examining how your past influences your future is critical. It helps you navigate through difficult times, but you have to take heed to what you've learned and then be willing to make the necessary adjustments to change the course of your life.

I once started a new relationship with someone who had several children. It was another blended family situation and another bad decision that I should have recognized right away. I was focusing on the love I had to give rather than the love I should be receiving. So, there I was loving, serving, and doing what I do best yet getting no return on my investments. We had only passed the six-month mark in our relationship when I once again began feeling discouraged. I knew there was something else I should be doing with my life. Deep down inside, I had very high standards for what I wanted in a wife. The way I was living was not on that level. I wanted more. One morning, I woke up early and I said to myself, "why am I in this relationship knowing she is unworthy of my love." I found contentment in being a provider for her and her children. Other than that, it was not a good situation. The tendency of unfortunate situations oscillated between one bad extreme to another. In my heart, I knew I was merely settling. In the best interest of all involved, I realized it was time for me to move on. The relationship lasted through Thanksgiving and Christmas. With the start of the New Year, I longed for a spiritual pendulum to take me back to my old roots. I needed to experience spiritual growth and healing to free me from the place of personal destruction. I had to stop running and surrender to God and His plans for my life. I no longer made pacts with myself, but I realized that to love as hard as I do, I already have the main ingredient needed—Jesus! Now it was time for me to follow His lead. I made a complete turnaround and I did not look back. This was the beginning of my spiritual journey.

HER

*Go to the One Whom the
Winds and Waves Obey*

J was very observant as a child, and I quickly learned what to do and what not to do. I wanted to go to college. My great grandfather told me "that ain't for us." He told me that Lincoln freed the slaves, but he left us with NOTHING. He said that college was "for people who had the means to go to college." I said, "I am going anyway." I would look out of the front door and see a lot of things in the project homes that did not fit me. My brain would observe things that were so clear to me and I couldn't understand why these things were constantly being repeated. That is why I became class president and a leader at an early age. I was standing up in class telling classmates "y'all better shut up because we got a test tomorrow and I'm getting an A."

My relationship with my mom has always been special in ways only she and I could understand. I always honored my mom through her times of weakness; although I did not always understand the choices she made and the circumstances she put us in while she was a very young mother herself. That all changed over time and our relationship has developed into a special mother-daughter friendship. She would say, "you know I did the best I could at the time." She told me, for the most part, she was in survival mode, and even when it may not have made sense for her to do some of the things she chose to do, she only did what she knew to do. During her moments of confession, she said she was suddenly realizing what childhood must have been like for me.

For most of my life, alcohol was the enemy. My grandmother was an alcoholic. Sometimes my mother would drop us off in the morning as she was going to school or work. She would be our sweet, gentle grandma when she opened the door, but within a moment she had her mixed orange juice by her chair ready to sip. We knew what would unfold before long. By the time my mom picked us up, my grandmother was extremely drunk (beyond coherency). I was just a little girl, but I was wise to watch everything around me. My discernment was high even then. By the end of the day, she would transform into a monster. She started cursing everybody out, staggering, falling, and peeing all over herself.

In her early days, my mom had her bouts with drinking alcohol, too. The neighborhood bar would call me and say, "Darlene, your mom is down here and has had too much to drink. Can you get somebody to come get her?" Here I am, a kid getting this phone call from a bartender (who was also a neighbor) asking me to find somebody to come get my mom. Being the oldest sibling, it was during these times, I felt a very heavy burden to protect my sisters and brother at all costs. Life was very serious to me. Alcohol was like the devil because I experienced firsthand what happened when someone consumed alcohol, and the turmoil it placed on me as a child. When I was raising my kids, I was serious about making sure no alcohol was ever allowed in my house. Now, my kids drink as adults and have expressed that they like that they can have an occasional drink with me.

The marriage relationship is God's perfect way of removing isolation and self-centeredness between two people. The replacement for selfishness is called oneness, which allows a couple the ability to create something together that could not exist with them apart. It is God's provision to meet our deep longing for close, intimate relationships through companionship in marriage. In this companionship, I believe its purpose is to also mutually meet each other's needs so that they in turn complete one another. I longed for this in my relationship. Yet, I lived on the edge of loneliness and total isolation throughout my entire twenty plus years of marriage.

Marriage suits me. I got married knowing that God's design for marriage is to create a conduit that serves to demonstrate His love for us through serving one another. I was intended to be that wife. I knew my marriage was not a function of God's design for our family. My strength to endure for so long came from my relationship with God. Nothing stopped me from trying to make something out of what I felt were just pieces of a dream. When God gave me the courage to be honest with myself, I found the strength to call out everything in my marriage that was not according to His design. No more pretending. I had to be honest with how I had been feeling for years. Proof that I was not operating out of a flimsy desire for personal happiness was that I had been suppressing the pain and disappointment early on in my marriage. I wanted to escape so that I could discover who I am outside of being in an unsatisfying marriage.

Confronting deep issues in my marriage was difficult. I tried everything in the book to make my marriage work. When my efforts fell short, I resolved that keeping my peace was the next best option. That was all I knew to do. Naturally, close friends and family were not surprised by my decision to divorce. Many of them knew of some of my struggles. They also knew that I was a strong woman who was not easily defeated by trials. We are living during a time when marriage is devalued and minimized. I never felt that way. I believe in marriage. In fact, when I was a young wife, I mapped out my idea of what a perfect marriage would look like. I have no regrets about being married. I just knew that this marriage was not what God had for me. He never intended for me to be devalued, feel constantly lonely and trapped, and emotionally abandoned. He loves me too much for that.

No one begins their marriage with an end in mind. I married at the young age of just 19 years old. I chose to marry because I had a child and refused to raise children without a dad. I experienced what that was like for myself and others and believed the best chance for success for children was to have their dad in the house. We had three beautiful children and life was good, or so I thought. My children mean the world to me. I poured my life into everything pertaining to my children. I had no time for diverting any energy into things that would make me happy, although I tried to make the best of my marriage for my children. My happiness depended on their happiness. As long as my children wanted for nothing, it was more satisfying to me than having a happy marriage. They did not ask to come into this world. But, the years of loneliness hurt so deeply it was starting to feel like physical pain. I was loyal to my children and the idea of keeping our family intact. For me, it was worth my suffering in silence for the best outcome for my children, especially while they were so young. No relationship is free from conflicts and disagreements. I consider myself strong and resilient. I am not one to run away at the first sign of discomfort. However, there could be hard moments in life that could stop you dead in your tracks. In relationships, it can make you feel even more vulnerable once you realize the given outcome is not left totally on you. When you are faced with making difficult decisions, it is a time that will require you to show up in ways that are uncomfortable. It takes courage blended with faith and truth to step up to the plate to deal with deep-seated issues.

It only took a couple of years into my marriage before I realized my marriage was not really a marriage at all. I remember once when my children were in grade school, I thought about *myself* for the first time ever. I felt like I raised my sisters and my brother, raised my children, and most of my family. After years of taking care of everyone else and making sure their needs were met, I assumed being married meant there would be someone to finally take care of me. Most of the time I felt lonely, unloved, used, and downright spent. The overwhelming feelings of emptiness and loneliness were unbearable. At that time, I felt walking away from my marriage would be selfish. Literally, it would mean depriving my children of growing up in a stable family with both parents. I made the decision, if he was not being abusive to me or the kids, it was important to me to have their dad around. Divorce was not an option. I felt stuck. Sometimes unexpected changes or misfortunes can be overcome through resilience. My ability to recover quickly from trouble and to bounce back kept me indebted to my marriage much longer than my heart was willing to hang on to it. I know I overcome through my resilience. When the hits come, I lean on the ropes and cover up. After all, resilience is primarily about mental strength. I was often feeling depressed serving others in ministry from a deficit. I buried myself in my work and church ministry. At times, I was spread so thin between taking care of my children, my job, and ministry, I knew my friends and family were praying me through. Going to church was very therapeutic for me. I was rejuvenated while working at the church and I looked forward to hugs and smiles. It refueled me to take on what I had to deal with during the week ahead.

I built for my family's benefit an entire enterprise; a safety zone so to speak. I realized how difficult it would be to isolate my issues in marriage from the health of the enterprise, but I came to a point where I could no longer ignore the fact that something needed to be done. After my kids were all out of the house, I knew I needed time to pour into myself. I took a year off work after working steadily for 25 years and entered counseling to make sure I was physically, emotionally, and spiritually healthy. I was having fun hanging out and doing what I chose to do. At this point, something inside wanted to scream with excitement. I felt so free. Life had finally quieted down for me. It was Darlene's time. I did not want any baggage. I did not want any drama. It was time to live my own life.

I always believed in how beautiful love could be but honestly, I had no faith to believe that kind of love would happen for me. I knew I had love to give, but I did not believe I could find someone to love me the way I knew I needed to be loved. I was just happy to exhale and experience freedom, happiness, and joy! I would attend social gatherings with my girlfriend Frannie and the "Chester folks" who were all living in Atlanta. It felt great to experience love and acceptance from bedrock friends who had known me and my family from childhood. When we all get together, it feels like life on wheels. We pick right up from the last time we were together no matter how long we had been apart. Our time together never gets old. At this time, I felt detached and not bogged down with anything. Life was good. No more drama. This was my time.

Being in this new, happy place was very unfamiliar. At times, I felt guilty for spending time doing whatever I wanted. I would have talks with myself mostly to make sure I was properly processing my thoughts and feelings. Should I be enjoying myself, I thought, and not thinking about anyone else except Darlene? What will everyone think of me now? Will I still be admired for taking such good care of my family? What will I lose in the process? It felt weird, but I was willing to trust God through the process. There were times it was difficult to explain why I looked so happy after walking away from a 25-year marriage. I was free from the pressure of having to do it all, while not having a safe place in my own home that I could go to be refueled. I talked less about it because who would truly understand it anyway. After all, I made marriage and family look beautiful. My children looked like the board of health, inwardly, outwardly, and spiritually. I poured my entire being into making sure my children did not experience the lack I was feeling deep inside. No one knew or could understand the loneliness and emotional deprivation I quietly endured on a regular basis.

It was a long, rocky ride, but I could finally live for me. In the eye of the storms of life, I have learned to be still and remain in control emotionally. It is hard to be thrown to and fro when you are determined to stand strong and secure because you are fully aware of who you are and what you have to offer. I thank God for my strength.

Reflections

What events in your life serve as turning points for your life's direction?

Describe a time in your life when you had to be brutally honest with yourself and find the strength to make a change?

LOVE FOUND:
DESIRING TRUE LOVE

HIM

*God's Plans Are Bigger
Than My Plans*

ife is full of beauty and in it, you can find many beautiful, extraordinary creations. Sometimes you do not have to look too far to find them. You can find them when you look deep from within. When you believe in yourself, it is difficult to give up on yourself. When hard winds and high waves try to overtake your life, you may not be able to stop the waves, but you can learn to surf in the direction of your dreams. My dreams and aspirations are what keeps me going. When I have something to believe in, it makes pressing toward my dreams more likely despite any roadblocks. I promised that I would never give up on my dreams of a journey of love. The love you have in your family should be rock-solid, unlike any other love you could ever experience in the world. The love I found in Darlene is unlike any love I have ever experienced in my life. This love felt like it was for me and I felt safe to give it my all. Knowing what it felt like to be loved by my mother and father growing up made me secure as a man. I used to dream about how I would love my wife and my family with all my heart. I always desired to have a Godly legacy; to love and serve my wife as Christ loves us all. In a marriage, I wanted the kind of love that requires the teamwork of a selfless, spiritual-minded husband and wife. As scripture says in Genesis 9:11, "God blessed them (the couple) and said for them to be fruitful (in the things of God) and multiply (his teaching) in the earth." This calls for marriages that draw positive attention to God through our lifestyles and how we love one another. I understood these types of roles in marriage can be taught in theory, but they are better taught by revelation within the marriage relationship. They are caught by revelation.

Through all my life experiences, heartaches, and disappointments, the one thing I do not regret is how I was always able to care for and serve people. I could take hard hits, but whenever I was knocked down, I did not stay down for too long. Being the oldest in my family, my brother and sister looked up to me and I never wanted to let them down. There are definitely things I would change about my past, but for the most part, I believe that what I learned through those bad experiences helped me to land on my feet today. Through the failed family life and my previous marriage, the separation from my father, and then his passing, I still have a heart full of love. I never gave up on the dream that one day I would find the woman of my dreams and I will spend my entire life making sure that she had everything pertaining to happiness at her fingertips. That is why I was so sure and adamant once I laid eyes on Darlene, that she was the one I wanted to spend the rest of my life with. The Bible says, "He who finds a wife finds a good thing and obtains favor from the Lord." (Proverbs 18:22) I found her and favor followed me to make having her possible. I needed His direction, guidance, and strength to make it happen because Darlene was no easy catch. She was way out of my league, but God said I could have her, so I was going to get my prize.

HER

Love Is Not What You Say—It's What You Do

e hear so much about the small word love. What is love? Is it the most amazing feelings you get from someone or is love strong feelings of affection that you have toward someone else? I knew what love should look like. Your inward feelings and body indicators will tell you a lot about your thoughts and interests. When you constantly find yourself pushing away your interests and what makes you feel satisfied for the interests of others, then that is a clear indication that the relationship is not healthy. If you pay attention to the indicators like your feelings and physical cues, it will help you develop the needed awareness so that you are not overlooking the most important person, which is you. These are the valuable lessons I learned through my first marriage. Stepping back from it now, I see that not only had I neglected myself, but I was also missing out on the true love and happiness that I always desired. I knew what I needed to be happy, although it ran much deeper than happiness.

After a few years into an empty marriage, I wrote a journal entry. The title said *True Relationship Happiness Means That All Major Needs Are Fulfilled.* On that page, I described all the major qualities that I felt were important for my husband to possess so that I would have a healthy and satisfying relationship. Clearly, I knew what I was missing but after years of neglect, I began to press these desires way to the back of my mind so that my heart could continue to pump love. The kind of love that is not just with words or speech but with actions and in truth.

The key to leading with love is knowing your worth and understanding what you have to offer. When you understand your value, you will understand who you are and the difference you can make in someone's life. Giving of myself so freely helped me to not be selfish, but it also taught me that to be a true leader, you must win the hearts of those who would be willing to follow. My drive and future aspirations were created during those moments when I would spend hours wondering how to put myself in a financial position to care for my family. I was always one with wisdom beyond my age. I grew up fast because I had no choice. My siblings needed me and I owned my reality.

Even though my siblings and I are close in age, I took pride in being supportive and caring for them. They looked to me for guidance, advice, and attention. Each of these leadership roles came to me naturally. It almost felt like leading was a perfect fit for my personality. I learned what it's like to be relied upon, so I would also try to do my best to give more than was required of me so that I did not come up short and let either of my siblings down. Something they understood but did not take for granted.

I clearly remember a season when my mother went into the military, which left no adults in the home. My mother's checks would come in the mail. I am not happy to admit this, but there were times I would forge her name on checks and find a ride to the grocery to buy food. There was no other choice. I would call a family member to take me to the supermarket where my mom had a store account. I could take her check there and they would cash it for me to purchase groceries. I was never a kid. I was in the 10th grade and an adult at home cooking and caring for my siblings. My sister, Freda, would clean the kitchen. My sister, Peanut, would sweep the floors. We kept everything at home in check. I do not remember having a Christmas. I remember a couple of times putting together my little brother's bike. I was responsible for a lot of things involving a lot of people. If something went wrong, it was my behind getting beat. It did not matter who was responsible for it. Everything was all on me just because I was the oldest.

My growing up was all work with very little time for play. Life was serious. I learned to calculate every dime. I needed to get in front and tell the dollars where to go and then not look back saying what happened when the money needed replenishing. Everything was calculated. I was diligent with directing where money should go and knew the purpose for every dollar that was spent. If I needed $5, I had no one who could help me. People would ask me for money but if I were in need, there was no one I could ask for money. I kept good track of my money and my spending to make sure everything was covered between paychecks. I was not dropping any balls; lights were not getting turned off. I had a lot on my shoulders at a young age.

For most of my life, just living equaled work and responsibility. Life was HARD for me, and I felt alone through most of it.

REFLECTIONS

What "bad" experiences were fuel for a bigger plan?

_____

_____

_____

_____

_____

_____

Was there a bigger plan that God had for you which required you to stretch? What was that plan?

_____

_____

_____

_____

_____

_____

Explain a time when you had to push away or push down your interests for the interests of others?

_____

_____

_____

_____

_____

Who Is She? – The Pursuit

HIM

*My Search for Darlene Led Me
to Finding True Love*

Somewhat like Darlene, I was also in a twenty-plus years marriage. I was not necessarily doing the right things to stay in the marriage. She was not educated. She did not have the tools necessary to raise children, but yet she was having a lot of children. I got caught up in that lifestyle. I was taking care of my kids and her kids too. I put myself in this situation. But I felt stuck. Then with her falling into severe drug addiction, it accelerated the deterioration of the whole marriage. I was to a point where I could not do this anymore. I told her that I was not going to watch her kill herself. I'm not going to say any more about that, but I was done with the marriage. At this point, it became a search for a new relationship. It did not become a Godly search until a couple of events happened to me. I was finding women in the wrong places. I was still doing some of the same unsmart things thinking it was going to be a drastic change but ultimately things ended similar to what I was running from.

The first time I encountered Darlene it was during one of those events where folks from Pennsylvania and Georgia connected. It was around April or May when we first met. Folks were getting together at a hole in the wall club where they played old school music and we would dance the night away. That is when I first laid eyes on Darlene and there was a fire that rose in me. It seemed to me that God was saying to me "there she is." There is the one I was looking for. It was like an out of body experience. We talked a couple of times during that evening. We were talking and we were kind of talking face to face and I got a chance to look into her eyes and something sizzled and burned right through my retinas. I could not keep focused on anything else except Darlene.

From that day forward, I was looking for Darlene to show up everywhere. It was like tunnel vision. The search went on for a while. I didn't even know Darlene. Here it is we are both from Chester, yet we had never met. After that first meeting, there was a big pursuit for Darlene. She just disappeared off the map. I had to track her down to let her know what I was feeling.

It was a long time before I saw her again. I found out that she had been dating someone and could already be in a relationship. I knew nothing about her relationship at that time. Every time an event came up, I was blowing up her friends' phone. BJ was the one who told me details about her. He shared with me that Frannie and Darlene were very close friends. They were classmates. It became a great big pursuit for me. I was blowing Frannie's phone up telling her to make sure Darlene comes to the next event. I wanted to see her so bad. I wanted to get to know more about her.

Prior to this pursuit, I experienced a spiritual awakening. I was coming out of this AHA moment with God. It was a significant turning point in my life. It was a spiritual transition for me. I got heavily involved in my church. At this moment in my life, it all came down to whether or not I was going to be a believer, change my lifestyle, and become the man God wanted me to be. I knew this would mean that all my old ways of thinking and my actions would have to be different. I was grateful for the spiritual experience and I was ready for the change. I could not find Darlene until I found my true self. I had to draw from my foundation and remember all the teachings I had from my Catholic experience and my experience from those summers I spent at my grandmother's church. I found a mentor to walk me through and hold me accountable. I had a real encounter with the Holy Spirit. Even now, it is hard to fully explain that experience in a way that would make sense to anyone. Subsequent to my spiritual encounter, I did not look the same. There was a noticeable difference in my life, and I did not care what people close to me thought of it. I was not turning back. God is real, and he showed himself to me. They would institutionalize me if I fully described my experience. The prayers that I prayed were really strong in me.

I would ask God to deliver me. This was really spiritual for me because I was seeking God and I believed he told me I could have Darlene. I prayed for his help to get to where I needed to be. I prayed prayers such as please don't let me mess up this lady's life. I remember going to sleep at night at home after the hour of time she would give me. She was on my mind. I remember that prayer was constant. Please let me get this right. Please don't let me mess this up. God, please give me the necessary tools. Please give me the resilience and courage that I need. Please help me, Lord. These were sincere prayers that I used to pray every day. As it turned out, this was a critical decision that I made at the best time of my life. I realized this time of unease and finding my way was for me to overcome in preparation for my journey to Darlene. It prepared me mentally for marriage with Darlene. When I first laid eyes on her, it was love at first sight. There was just something special about Darlene. I saw new possibilities with her that I never thought possible. I kept an open mind about all the possibilities.

HER

Discover Who You Are—Know Your Value

*H*ave you ever asked yourself, "Who am I, really?"' Truth is, we all have multiple identities and sometimes one could be meaningfully dependent on the other. For example, I am a mother. I have a mother. I am her daughter. I have daughters, and so on. We are a summation of the family we grew up with, our experiences, and our environments. We hold distinct separate roles within each of our relationships. Keeping this in mind helped me to avoid losing sight of myself while providing for the needs of other important relationships in my life. Thinking of yourself first is not selfish. I came to realize that it is necessary. When we learn of ourselves, we can grow and develop in any situation. We learn about ourselves through our relationships and from the world we see around us. The best way to learn about yourself is to not be afraid to comb through your life and to peel back the layers, which is what I had to do during the process that led to my divorce. I feel very passionate about this now because in my previous marriage I rarely gave myself much thought.

In celebration of my transformation after my divorce, I began spending time with myself. I took myself out on dates. Got a gym membership and started routinely spending several days a week developing routines that I would enjoy. Aqua-fit turned out to be my favorite. I took aqua classes several times a week. At this point in my life, I thought I'm good; no drama. I had raised everyone and now I had the experience of being on my own. My children were grown and out of the house. It is now my time.

I started dating a guy that we called the seven-footer because of his height. We dated for almost a year. I called this a time for me to explore Darlene. Initially, we had been spending a lot of time together. My class reunion was coming up and I invited him to accompany me to the reunion. He agreed to accompany me. By the time we returned to Atlanta, the relationship did not feel right to me anymore. Over the summer, things started going haywire. His mom had passed away and we weren't seeing much of each other. He was not available to me as much physically or emotionally. I suggested that we step back and take a break. Let's take a 30-day break and decide what this is going to be for us and let's figure out where we go from here. As time went by, I realized this was not the relationship God had for me. I do not know how to be half in and half out with my commitment. I noticed that I started holding back my feelings, my efforts, my time, and my ideas. This was an unfamiliar place for me. I was either all the way in or not. I was not into anyone being so reserved with their efforts, so the break was quick and final.

Frannie called to invite me to a gathering, which I attended alone. I was excited about the opportunity to get away. Turns out this gathering was a birthday party. Billy says this is when he saw me the second time. That is also when I heard from many that Billy had been looking for me. When I recalled who he was, I remember thinking "oh, that's that loud guy." Whenever he walks in, everybody would start throwing up shots as if he was the life of the party.

Enjoying adult functions alone actually felt good! I was having the time of my life. I probably had never gone to one bar back in the City of Chester. I was not on that scene. I got married at 19 years old and by 21 I had two kids, and my great grand-mother to care for while working a full-time job at a local bank. I was in a marriage where my ex-husband felt like my fourth child. My hard work and dedication paid off at home and work. I consistently worked hard even getting a promo-tion at work to further my career up the corporate ladder.

So, we were at this party where Billy finally saw me again after several months. I saw him staring down at my hands. He said "I like your nails. They look nice. Would you like some-thing to drink?" He was saying things to me oftentimes as he was passing by. He was very attentive and so bold in trying to serve me. He was always so loud. It seemed like his loudness woke up the party. I thought to myself now that I was finally free, I was not willing to wrap myself up in any drama. But something was intriguing about his lively personality. I briefly wondered what it would be like to spend time with him and his extremely outgoing demeanor.

He tried several times to approach me, but each time I told him I don't have time for drama, and I have no time to waste on foolishness! He finally said, "so you are not even going to give me a chance?" I told him with a stoned face that he has just one hour. I thought that would throw him off but instead, he stated one word, "Bet!" I chuckled at his unexpected response; he smiled and again said "Bet." When I initially suggested to Billy that I would give him one hour, I meant that I would give him one hour on any given day, and that's it! It was as if Billy either did not understand that I meant just "one" day, or he completely ignored the fact that I said I would give him "one hour to see what he was about." He was so consistent every day with getting his hour that I wanted to remind him of the agreement, but by our third or fourth day, I was intrigued by how much thought he was putting into our times of connection. He was so delighted every day just to spend time with me.

My father and grandfather were very affectionate. They used to say to me "if your husband does not know how to grab you, smack you on your behind, and love all over you, you better find someone who can." Trying so hard to be the young Christian wife, I would feel embarrassed. I would say "y'all cannot be telling me this kind of stuff." Dad and granddad used to love me with a deep love. They demonstrated to me what it felt like to be truly valued and cherished. They treated me like I was the jewel of the family. I felt like they would dive to the bottom of the ocean for me. I knew the kind of love they had for me. They knew I was not getting the love, attention, and affection I needed at home for all I was pouring out for the entire family. They knew I was not getting it back. I was wrung out, tired and it was beginning to show. They wanted something better for me so there is a bit of a spiritual aspect to this. I believe that what I see in Billy is what they sent for me. Everything they said to me about what they wanted for me before they died, I see in Billy. I believe they sent him to me. First, he had to be cleansed. Billy still had quite a bit of that roughneck personality, but he had to mature to a place where he would not destroy my life.

My journey with Billy started from the first day he said "bet." He came to my house every day looking for his one hour. Every day we spent together we would talk about things for hours. As I would talk, he was the perfect gentleman waiting for me to finish my thoughts without interrupting. This act of consideration let me know he was really listening to what I was saying rather than waiting for his turn to talk. He let me know he was grateful for the hour and it showed. Every single day he came to my house and said, "Come on out, get in the car, and fasten your seat belt." That statement was said to me every day. I did not know what to expect because each time, Billy had all the plans well thought out in every single detail. My only responsibility was to come out, get in his car, and fasten my seatbelt!

There is great significance to 'Get in the car, fasten your seat belt' if you think about our lives. You may not know where you are going, but you can trust and believe that your destination will be safe and satisfying. This requires trust and faith that you will be safe and you will be well taken care of. But for me, it also meant giving up control to someone else. I did not have the plan! This, in and of itself, was new territory for me.

Every moment I spent with him was divine. He put me in and out of the car, held my hand, and carried every bag as he took me somewhere every day for one hour. Billy would say let's go here and get a slice of pizza. Let's go get an ice cream cone. Billy's hour was simple but always very pleasurable. I remember one date was on a Tuesday. He picked me up and said, "It's Crab Leg Tuesday." So, that is what we did. He took me to have some crab legs and we ate and enjoyed one another's company. It was really nice.

On one date, he said let's get a hamburger; on another, he packed a picnic and took me to the park. We had a little picnic on his blanket as we laid out in the sun. He was a perfect gentleman. He had a lot to talk about. He had never touched anything other than my hand. That day while we were at the park, I was wearing my favorite sundress. As I was laying on my stomach, he lifted my sundress to take a peek and then quickly pulled it back down. It seemed to me as if he was making sure that I didn't have butt pads on or something. But I could tell he liked what he saw by the smile on his face and the look in his eyes.

Still, he was a perfect gentleman and we talked a lot during his one hour. I realized that this man was quick-witted and very intelligent. He used a couple of words that I did not know the meaning of, although I wouldn't tell him that I didn't know what they meant. I was impressed when I learned he had a Catholic school education. He was a super smart student and made good grades. He knew a lot of things about a lot of topics. He was kind of nerdy; and I joked that he was filled with endless, useless information!

For example, one day we were driving under a tunnel and he was admiring the structure. He said let me tell you how tunnels are made. Have you ever thought about how tunnels are made? Then he proceeded with his lesson. They dig a hole and they take in the dirt and they recycle it in this machine that mixes it with a cement compound. After it reaches a specific consistency, it spits it back out while continuing to dig holes. I said "Okaaayyy?!?!" He was knowledgeable about nerdy things that I never even think about. Navy experience creates discipline, but he was also light-hearted and fun. I learned a lot about his Navy background. He has a knack for learning new things and he is very educated. He was always upbeat. I've never seen a frown on his face. He is always accommodating and never complains about anything, even though sometimes I thought there were times he should. Such as, I would say "oh no we are not going to accept that" and he would calmly and simply say "it's ok." He has a way of bringing me such calm.

As you would imagine, all of this is new to me because I had a negative person in my life and the differences could not be more glaring. Every day for two months he got his hour without interruptions. I would notice little things like if I were running late and needed an extra ten minutes, Billy would come inside to patiently wait for me as I was finishing up. I remember thinking, did that man just clean my dishes while I was getting dressed? One time, I had some towels in a basket that I had taken out of the dryer. I noticed he had neatly folded all of my towels. There was another time he started cleaning up the dog food that Chester spilled on the floor before I could even get to it. He would do all these things before I even realized they were being done. I never had to ask nor would I have thought to ask him to do any of those things. I could tell it was his pleasure to serve.

REFLECTIONS

List something you discovered that you truly needed but did not realize until after you found it?

_____

_____

_____

_____

Have you ever been consumed with pursuing something? What was it? What drove your pursuit?

_____

_____

_____

_____

Name something you have had to settle within yourself before engaging in healthy relationships with others?

_____

_____

_____

_____

Have you made yourself just as important as everyone else in your life? Describe some of those times.

_____

_____

_____

_____

WINDOW OF OPPORTUNITY

HIM

Opportunity Never Passes
the Right Person

Throughout my life, I realized that there has always been a sense of knowing God is with me. I sense his grace, protection, and guidance in my life through the good times and the bad. However, all of the forces of darkness cannot stop God's plans for my life. He does not change his mind about us no matter what our lives look like to others. With this awareness, I recognized that through my journey of finding and loving Darlene, I believe a large part of it was answered prayers that I had prayed to God to let me have Darlene. I would have gone to any measure to make this dream a reality. I prayed and asked God to give Darlene eyes for me. I prayed when He did, that he would help me not to mess it up. When I first laid eyes on Darlene, I could not get her out of my mind.

When we finally met, we were both already in a relationship with someone else. God had to create an opportunity for us to get together. I had been with this girl for six or seven months. We met on the internet. It was obvious we were not compatible but for me, it was just something to do to numb me from my pain and disappointments from my failed marriage. Her oldest daughter's graduation was approaching. We had been discussing the activities and expenses for the graduation together when I noticed something I had not seen before. While I was willing to spend money to help out with the graduation, I realized she had not once involved or even mentioned asking the child's dad for any support. She had three young children with him, yet he was not involved with the eldest or the youngest child. The middle daughter enjoyed a relationship with her dad, but the others had practically none. The oldest daughter and her mom were butting heads like two rams. It came time for her oldest to graduate from high school. I sat down with her daughter to talk about what fees were coming due and to figure out how we were going to put our money together to get her a class ring. Senior dues and payments for her cap and gown were also coming due. We took out a pen and paper to write it all out. I encouraged her that we were going to take care of everything and she had nothing to worry about. In the end, I pretty much took care of all the costs myself. It was important to me not to see her disappointment from not having what she needed for graduation. One night the phone rang and her daughter's father was on the other end of the phone. We were sitting close to each other at the time, which allowed me to overhear their conversation. He said something about picking up the middle daughter again on Sunday. This was something he often did on Sundays, but he did not include any of the other girls. When she got off the phone, it hit me again that she had not bothered to even ask him for the money to help out with his daughter's graduation expenses. Then, I decided to ask her about it, and she said to me "You know how he is." First of all, I do not know him, so I immediately responded "No, I do not know how he is." Her strong southern dialect often caused her to repeat herself to me and honestly, I could not understand what she was saying half the time. When we visited her mom's house, they would be sitting there talking loudly. Most of the time, I struggled to make out the gist of their conversations. That was my first red flag that this relationship would not fare well. I realized how different we were in personality and lifestyle. It sounded like a different language to me. It was during this time that I began to ask the Lord to create moments for change for my life. That is when I met and began to pursue Darlene. Just as the pursuit started, God started to create space and opportunity for us.

I was not aware of it at the time, but Darlene had already put her relationship on pause for 30 days. I began to unravel from my relationship. After that incident happened, I started packing my stuff and keeping it neatly tucked away out of sight. I began subtly pulling all my clothes out of my drawers and putting them away in suitcases. I would go out on weekends looking for an apartment so that I could move on. I had decided that I was leaving the relationship. I could no longer waste time if I was seriously asking God who He had especially for me. I made the mistake of staying around too long in my previous marriage even though I knew the relationship had ended. This time I was not willing to make that mistake twice. It was time for me to move on. By this time, I am out of the relationship and Darlene had paused her relationship. I had moved out. Ironically, we both knew that it was not working out with the person we were with. Turned out, we were both cutting old ties and preparing for a long road ahead of true love, fulfillment, and happiness at the same time.

HER

*Extraordinary Comes to Those
With Great Expectation*

*C*onfidence is being sure of what we hope for and having the patience to wait for it and trusting God during the process. Oftentimes, when we know our value, we expect that everything we believe we deserve we should receive. I am always one who has great expectations. When I see something that I want, I go after it hard and focus on it until I get it.

With Billy, he made it clear from day one that he understood the value in me, which initially took me by surprise. While his previous relationship was unraveling, and he was figuring out what direction he would take, my relationship was on pause while I did the same. My life was peaceful and quiet. I was drama-free and wanted to remain that way. The kids were out of the house. It felt divine. I was not trying to raise anybody else. I was not trying to change anyone into a person they were not. All I wanted to do at this point was to define what I wanted and what I did not want in my life. I decided that anything that did not bring me peace or add value, I would not make time for. This is why without hesitation I told Billy, "You have only one hour; I do not have time to waste!" My time was valuable.

Spending time with Billy brought back to my mind when my father and grandfather would talk to me about what I was missing out on in life. They would tell me that I was a special lady and that I needed someone who valued me and treated me with the utmost respect and honor that I deserved. I strongly believe they have a lot to do with Billy and me being together today. When I look at pictures of my father and grandfather, they look a lot like what I see in Billy. They were loud and wild just like Billy. They were very street smart. Although dad spent a lot of time getting high, robbing, and stealing, they were fun and filled with laughter whenever I was around them. My grandfather was called Clean Head in the streets of Philly. He was always suited up with a hat, suit, and dress shoes. Even if he wasn't going anywhere, he would sit on the sofa with his hat right next to him. He frequented the number houses and loved to make moonshine. But I knew without a doubt, that they loved and cherished me. A lot of what I learned about being loved came from what they showed me about what loving me should look like, sound like, and feel like. They helped me think about and mentally understand what I should expect in a man. I believe daddy and granddaddy sent Billy to love and care for me in the way they wanted me to be loved.

The one hour with Billy showed me the importance of being with someone who thinks enough of me to map out every detail just to spend time with me. I never knew where we were going for that one hour. He allowed me to dial back my brain because someone else was using theirs and I liked that. From the moment I told Billy that he has one hour, in my mind, I was wondering if this was a too-good-to-be-true moment. He was so genuine and focused on doing the work to make me smile. Those one-hour moments added up to hours of spending my time with someone who valued my time just as much as I valued his. Still, I continued to emphasize that we were not dating, even though I was beginning to look forward to spending time with him. When we were not together, I would start missing our time and I wondered what he was planning for our next hour. By this time, I was feeling like it was time to let down my guard just a bit. I gave Billy a new name that only I could call him. His friends and family called him Bilal. I told them that Bilal was not husband material so I changed his name to Sweet William.

It was summer now and I was really liking how I was beginning to feel. I was looking forward to spending time with Billy with the excitement of wondering what was the next place he would take me. In the evening, right around 7:00 p.m., you would find me literally sitting at the window looking and waiting for him to come. He was always on time so I knew I would not be waiting long before he pulled up and gestured to me to come out. It was the most exciting time of my day.

We enjoyed talking for hours and he would always hang onto my every word. If I ever said I like something or I would like to have something, he would make a mental note of it. Before long, he would either get it for me or make sure I experienced something that I said I wanted. There were certain things that I said lightly in conversation that he acted upon. For instance, I remember when my nephews were visiting me hanging out in my backyard all summer long. My nephews love to come and hang out, watch movies, or listen to music out in the backyard. After they had spent the entire summer at the house, when summer was coming to an end, everything was left out of place and things needed to be put back in place. They left the backyard a complete mess. Stuff was left everywhere. The backyard needed some serious attention and I had planned to get around to taking care of it soon. They left stuff leaning against the garage and the shed. One day while I was working from home, I was at the kitchen table working when I noticed Billy's van pull up on the side of my house. He did not knock on the door, so if I had not looked up and noticed the van in my yard, I would not have known he was there. He came to take care of business in the backyard and he stayed out there working for hours until everything was spotless. He cleaned up the entire yard. He even organized the shed which had been needing attention for years. He laid down some blue tarp on the ground and started pulling everything out of the shed to organize everything. There was no telling what was in there because stuff had been thrown in there over the years. He had been working for hours without even coming into the house. At one point, he looked up and waved hello. I waved back and he just kept at whatever he was doing. I wanted to at least bring him something to drink but he looked like he did not want to be interrupted. I guess I could have insisted he pause a moment to have something to drink, but quite honestly, I was in such a trance of what I was witnessing as I sat there in a daze. I had never seen a man work as hard and diligently in my life. After the backyard and the shed were spotless, he backed up the van and pulled off hauling away a van full of trash. I sat there for a while in complete amazement and disbelief. I was honestly floored.

The amount of time Billy and I were spending together was picking up steam. As Labor Day was approaching, I certainly did not think anything would be any different. I was spending a lot of time at the gym working out and being active outdoors. It was a time of refreshing in my life. We had been having so much fun spending all summer long together. The summer was over and I had not been to the beach at all. I love the water. I took aquafit classes, but that was different from going to the pool or being on the beach. In my mind, I thought if I could only go to the beach, that would make me very happy. I wanted sand between my toes but now the summer was over. It made me sad that I was feeling like I missed out on the summer. Billy refused me the opportunity to sulk about it. He was just content spending time together and making our time together feel special.

One early Saturday morning, I was surprised by a knock on the door because I was not expecting anyone. To my surprise, Billy was standing with a mischievous smile on his face. As he did every time he came for his one hour, he came in with his usual statement, "Get in the car and fasten your seat belt." By now, I had grown to love that statement because Billy brings his A-game and he never disappoints. I took no time getting my stuff together, grabbed my bag, and out the door we went. Most of the time I did not know where we were going beforehand, but I was eager to be going with him. Usually, I am known to have it all under control. I would typically have my entire year planned out. I know what I am doing today, next week, and next month. I could usually tell you where I am going to be next year. In my past experiences, if I didn't plan it, do all the leg work, make 1000 phone calls, it wasn't going to happen. I did not do anything that I did not plan out myself. It was draining. The very fact that I could get in the car and fasten my seat belt without knowing or having to ask is very indicative of the life that I have with Billy. It all started from those hours. This is a totally different experience for me so it was great to have somebody else making all the plans. For somebody else to use their brains to make things happen, meant that I could now dial my brain back a couple of notches. That felt so good. Somebody else can make all the calls and make all the arrangements. Somebody else got it and I didn't have to lift one finger. Before, I could not even really enjoy activities from being exhausted from having to think through how we are going to get from here to there. Do we have to have money for this? What are we not thinking about? My brain was always working trying to figure out everything myself, while not letting any balls drop. That's all gone with Billy. He has it covered so I can sit back and take in the moments with delight. Several times I would have to ask, where is my pocketbook? Of course, Billy would say, right here, I have it! My brain was able to relax and it was freeing.

At this point we had been driving for hours. Billy was deep, in thought , I was deep in thought. Suddenly , I realized we were in Savannah! Billy practically drove right on to the beach. He opened my car door and said, " Put your toes in the sand"!

Also, While in this window of opportunity, Billy was focused on praying and remaining in the presence of the Word. He constantly asked God for directions. I remember him telling me, "God already told me I could have you." I told him not to play the God-card with me and reminded him that God hadn't told me anything even though I was starting to feel that he was winning me over with his attentiveness to me. He listened to what I would say and if he thought something was bothering me, he would act upon it before I could even think about what was actually bothering me. He was listening carefully to hear my wants, needs, or desires so that he could meet them. Even today, I have to be careful about what I say. If I say I want something or want to try something, he would listen to me as if I was asking for it. Like the time when he brought home this perfume. He said, "Hey baby, you said you wanted this perfume." I asked him what the perfume was and when did I ask for it? He said once when I was watching the commercial for JADORE and said "Oh my God, I have to get some of that!" It just looked like it smelled good on the commercial. It looked like some good stuff. I was not planning on running out and purchasing it any time soon. Once it registers in his brain, if he can make it happen, you can consider it a done deal. I have to be careful if I say I want something because if it is in his power, he is going to make it happen.

In anticipation of the unknown of where exactly this genuine love could take me, I honestly stood in awe every day I spent time with him. Being so unfamiliar with this love, I think it may have put me on guard about going too fast too soon with our relationship. It ultimately caused me to embrace the idea of a forever love with this wonderful man with whom I was so happy to spend one hour.

REFLECTIONS

When have you found yourself at what we call the sweet spot—where your desires meet with the perfect opportunity?

_____

_____

_____

_____

Has there been a space created or door opened for just a period of time that would have closed had you not acted? Explain that window of opportunity.

_____

_____

_____

_____

Has there been a time when you set your expectation and did not budge from it? (ex. A price, a requirement, a time-frame or deadline.) What standards did you set?

_____

_____

_____

_____

_____

_____

YOUR WORDS PRODUCE
LIFE OR DEATH

HIM

I Know I Can Love Her

A man must first find himself before he finds his woman, or he will damage whatever woman he comes in contact with along the way. I was feeling quite good about the way things were going with me and Darlene. I was ready to make my move. I had been praying and believing it was the right time for me to step out on faith. It was risky for me to be praying for someone to be my wife before it was revealed to her that she was the one. Yet, it is exhilarating to see how things were unfolding. There were several reasons for my asking Darlene for just one hour. I had well-thought-out plans of all the wonderful things I wanted to do for her. The whole idea stemmed from my desire to search out her secret places that had not been tapped into for years. I could see in her eyes the vulnerable, precious soul longing to be loved. I knew that within every opportunity she allowed me to spend with her lied great possibilities for me to dig deeper to discover everything I needed to know about her so that I can make her live her best life. My mission would be to take care of her and to make sure she experienced a lifetime of vacations.

While I was watching and waiting, I told God that if he said, I had done enough, I would quit because I did not want to mess this up. I know how to run away. During this whole time of transition. I was starting to change into this confident, determined man. I was seeing some things differently. When you make someone know your true feelings and make them feel special, they, in turn, will invest in you more than you believe. This exchange becomes the building blocks for a solid foundation built on positive experiences and outcomes. All of these things became bigger than my fears and fueled trust in my faith and the promises of God. He turned my dreams for her into something that fueled my faith and my passion.

When I looked at Darlene, I would see a halo around her and I wanted that for me as well. I wanted to fall under that halo or even join our halos together to make something even brighter. It felt like our lights were immersed in each other such as if you took two flashlights and put the individual beams together so that you can't even see the lights coming together, but you can see a brighter illumination as they mesh together so perfectly. It is sort of like mixing sugar and butter to make a cake but the joining of the two is much more effortless.

I knew my party lifestyle filled with drinking and drugs all eventually needed to be discontinued. I wasn't necessarily hooked on any of it, but it was like a constant party. I could hide between various functions and actions, but the fact of the matter was that I was in love with Darlene. I was present in my reality of what needed to take place before I could marry someone like Darlene. This love was right for me because looking at Darlene I saw how us coming together would make a power-packed force to be reckoned with. As one, we could gel together so wonderfully! This is all starting to be seen as a fulfillment of God's promises. I believe that those life transformations that the Lord took me through led to the reality of a true love that was reachable and real as I watched our relationship unfold.

Listening to Darlene's life story from the beginning, I knew where she was coming from. We both were at a deficit in some areas. Ironically, we each have very different deficits, which makes it more possible for us to be strong where the other one may be weak. There was a yearning and crying out for more. Being able to have that shoulder to cry on was important for both of us. Darlene had a more feminine way of expressing herself but her emotions brought out a lot of my emotions. There was some relief in being able to share on a level with somebody that I could talk and relate to. I was here in Georgia alone so having someone real was key to me getting to a place where I was honest enough and vulnerable enough to follow guidance from God. At times, I felt very lonely, but loneliness during this season was necessary for me. It kept me from swaying from my heart's desire and from getting myself into any trouble.

Darlene understood me, and she could recognize where I was coming from in my situation. She could understand because we had the same culture and same background. That was huge for me. At that time, much of what I talked about was really me crying out. Even though I had made major changes in my life and was a different person on the inside, I was afraid that I would somehow fall into the same patterns as in previous relationships. That was not what I needed to do. Darlene was very, very different! I just needed to stay the course and be patient. Being able to identify with her even though we walked different paths let me know that God had a different plan for me. He had someone especially in mind for me.

I feel like Darlene was well out of my reach. My desire was to one day get there, by all means necessary, even though I was intimidated by her. I still am to some degree. I never had a woman of her caliber. I never had someone with her knowledge, skills, and intelligence. I have always been in what I called "captain save a hoe situations." As funny as it may sound, this was true for every relationship I ever had. I always found myself in that role almost instantly. Darlene is a lot different in so many ways from what I previously experienced. I went from the bottom of the barrel to the top of the mountain. Foothill to high hill. It was a challenge I was determined to take seriously. This was huge!

The Lord knew I could do it but he started me off right where he needed me to be. He required me to step up my game. I needed to do this and he did not give me any small tasks. It was more than what I could handle. It was a handful that I knew I could not handle on my own. He did not skimp on me. Everything that I was given was exactly what I asked for. God is true to his word and he had already begun revealing it to me. It was like the next step toward the next level. Walking in and stepping out on the promises. Those that I could see and even the ones yet to be revealed. I was confident that I could do this with every fiber in me. I know I will love her with everything in me. Now that I know I love her and that she is truly worthy of my love, that is exactly what I am going to do for the rest of her life.

HER

Be Specific! Speak It Into Existence

*Y*ears of journaling taught me to release and own my thoughts and feelings. I am a very self-aware person, so tapping deeply into my feelings is not difficult for me. Knowing and accepting my preferences, helped me understand myself during the lack of fulfillment in my marriage. It also helped me to map out how I saw a more acceptable future for myself. As I look back at some of those journal entries, it amazes me how I was able to exhibit so much grace and strength while going through 25 years of misery in marriage. I looked back at some of the things I wrote and how I was feeling at the time. A couple of journal entries, in particular, came to mind. In my 10th year of marriage, while I was feeling depressed and stuck, I always had a handle on my emotions. The entries during this time had themes such as this CANNOT be it for me! How did I get here? There was constant tension. I knew that God had formed me and made me the way that I am. Therefore, if I have needs, then God gave them to me. Should I change who I am and what I need to be fulfilled to accept unmet needs? Are my needs unrealistic? In a perfect world, I would have a husband who exhibits certain qualities and characteristics that make me feel safe, taken care of, and satisfied. I could not see how that would be asking for too much.

The characteristics I would desire in a partner formed the acronym "Pass Me." If he is not willing to provide for me in ways that are meaningful to me, then he could pass me. I would rather be by myself than be unhappy, unfulfilled, and trapped in a sad marriage.

Here are the characteristics and descriptions outlined in that journal entry:

Physical: There must be physical chemistry between us. Must love me, my body. Openly display affection, hands always on me letting me know he is there, and I am not alone. Love to hug, kiss, and cuddle all day. Privately must be passionate and intense. Must be able to satisfy me sexually.

Attitude: Must be a team player, cooperative, able to give praise and credit to others. Be friendly and open. Have no ego or insecurity hang-ups about himself. Extremely confident yet very open to learning, able to admit when wrong, admit when he has a lot to learn, able to say I'm sorry, must know how to ask for help, and must be able to cry.

Spiritual: Must be equal; both must love the Lord. Seeks God for direction, decision, etc. Openly praising, praying, and worshipping God. Leading the family to church; leading family worship and prayer. Praying for me and with me.

Social: Must be a strong communicator of feelings, thoughts, ideas, plans, goals, etc. Must have an outgoing personality and be talkative with everyone. Must love family, and gatherings, and must speak well. Must carry himself in a mature, responsible, and respectful manner. Must make me proud in front of others.

Mental: Must challenge me mentally in conversation. Must be quick, witty, precise, perceptive, and fun. Must have a positive philosophy about life, values, love, and faith. Must have personal goals and plans and know where he has been and where he wants to be. Must be mature and disciplined. Must always make good decisions, especially regarding money, jobs, investments, and spending.

Emotional: Must hurt whenever I hurt. Must "feel me." Must have a genuine concern for my needs. Must know how to read me. Willing to supply my emotional needs. Must freely compliment, support, nurture, and reassure me. Must pay attention to me. I have to be "everything" to him.

While dating Billy, I remembered I put together a list of my desires years ago during my years of sadness and discontentment. I went digging through my files and found the original copy of the list. I shared it with my girlfriends, and they said, "Darlene, you created Billy. You spoke him into existence!" I never thought of it that way, but I believe it to be true. I cannot even act like I knew what I was doing at the time I wrote the list, but I knew in my heart that despite what I was going through God wanted much better for his daughter. Honestly, it was probably written out of frustration from the deficit of just about everything on this list! I have learned to be specific with God as much as possible when asking for something–a job, an opportunity, etc. I am thankful to God for answering specific prayers; even ones that I had not mentioned or the ones that I may have even forgotten about!

REFLECTIONS

When have you wanted something so badly that you were willing to do whatever it takes, even a total life change, to get it?

Take steps this week to write an alternative positive reality for your life. Include what you want and what you have to do to get it.

PROFESSING MY LOVE

HIM

Confess the Love You Want.
You Can Have It!

nce I realized that I had what it would take to be the best husband for Darlene, I began to make note of everything I would do to make her the happiest girl in the world. I made promises to myself and God that I knew I must keep. At this point, I had gotten a lot of revelation and I figured out we had something special together. I realized I was already in love with Darlene so it was just a matter of convincing her that I was the one for her. I was giddy with excitement to finally get a chance to tell Darlene that I was in love with her from day one. It crossed my mind several times much earlier on to just tell her because it all felt so right. Fear of pushing her away if I moved too quickly was the only reason for not spilling it all by this point. It was important for me to remain deeply involved with spending time with God and staying in His word. I talked to God every step of the way. I desired to do everything that

God laid on my heart by listening for His voice and by not stepping out on my own. He showed me the kind of love that I could show Darlene and because He loves me, I know I can love Darlene the way she deserves to be loved. He told me to let all I do be done in love; and I promised I would do that in our marriage for the rest of my life. There were some real moments when I was discovering and admiring what I saw in Darlene inwardly. I discovered that she is really clean cut and she has a heart of gold.

I had planned to kidnap her for a day trip to Savannah that weekend. I dreamt that as soon as she put her blue toenails in the blue water (she was wearing blue nail polish on her toes), I would pour my heart out to her. That thought stayed on my mind the whole time while I was driving her to Savannah. As soon as I saw the ocean and all of that water that stretched far and wide, I saw it as all of the never-ending love I have for Darlene. A love that was so deep and wide it would never fade. Looking out at all the water, I felt like that is how much love I can give to her. Right there on the beach, while we were both immersed in the warm ocean water, I began to confess to her the love I have for her. I took her by the hand as I turned to her, looked into her eyes, and said, "I believe God said I can have you." I promised her that everywhere we go people will know about our love. They will see it, feel it and it will inspire people to love. People will have hope that true love is still possible. I was so sincere, and I meant every word that I shared. I will prove it to her every day of my life.

Darlene called the profession of my love for her that day in Savannah a "full speech." To me, it was not a speech at all. They were words that I peeled off my heart to share with her in their fullness. The entire three-hour ride from Atlanta to Savannah, all I could think of was the words that I was about to share and how she had no idea they were coming. This was the moment I was waiting for. I professed my love to Darlene expecting her to say nothing in return. All I wanted from her was to receive every word I shared in truth and love. This was the day that could be seen as the first day of the beginning of the rest of our lives.

After the excitement of the day's events, we ended up staying the night in Savannah. This was the first time we spent this kind of time together. Even still, she continued to remind me that I am not her "boyfriend." I just smiled. She didn't know what I knew. We took nice pictures while we were on the beach. She insisted that I not post any of the pictures of us on Facebook. She said that we are not together and she did not want our friends to think that we were. Darlene posted a picture of her beautiful toes in the sand with blue toenail polish. The post said, "Savannah - finally, my toes are in the sand." Within 60 seconds, her phone started ringing off the hook. Her girlfriend and roadie, Frannie, wanted to know why she was in Savannah without her and who she was with. This information took quite a while for her to digest; at this point, she had only limited knowledge of the time that we had been spending together every single day.

Like a ball rolling down the hill, there were so many obstacles that I encountered during this period. I overcame them all by walking it out with confidence. I remember the prayer that I prayed. Lord, please don't let me mess up this woman's life. I had family that she had not yet met. I was afraid of how it would turn out once she met them. I think I had her at this point, but I still was not 100% sure she was ready for all that it may take to be a part of my life. She did not know me in all of my stuff. She had no clue what she was walking into. I wasn't sure she would want it. I was afraid she would run the other way after learning about the sum of me and all of the twists and turns I had taken with my family. She was walking on a thin line of faith because she was experiencing the new and transformed Billy, but my past was far less pleasant. She was waiting for God to compel her, but I knew exactly what she was about to walk into. Meeting my family and revisiting my past was a part of the story that she needed to understand. So, one day I just asked her, "Darlene, will you go home with me?" I was feeling pretty good about having shared my feelings with Darlene. Clearly, I was so excited about having her in my future. We are both from the same hometown of Chester, Pennsylvania, although it was in Atlanta, Georgia where I first laid eyes on her. We met during a get-together with folks from our hometown. When I asked Darlene if she would go home with me for Thanksgiving weekend, her first response was, "NO WAY!" I explained that my class of '82 was having a 50th birthday party. I wanted to go home with her! She was my prize. So, I asked her to go. She looked as if she was about to die! She told me that her class of '83, all of her friends, all who knew her in Chester, and all of her family would jump all over her, and me too, if we popped up on them! Ohhh nooo! She could tell that I was a bit deflated by her answer and reaction. She must have continued to think about it because after a while she came back with a very calculated Darlene-type of response. "I'll tell you what," she said. "If come November 1st, I haven't had any red flags at that point, I will go with you to your class event." All I ever needed was a chance! Nothing excites me more than a challenge and I accepted this one!

I can honestly say that today, Darlene has a much better, more focused version of me. When the line was drawn, I had no intentions of turning back. No more riding the fence. All of that went out the window. The obstacles I had with alcohol and drugs by this time were no longer an issue. It was all off the table and out of my reach. Being with Darlene was like being at the apex of the mountain, and yet the foothill always had a spot in the back of my mind. My family included generations of drugs and alcohol. My grandkids became a huge part of my desire for change. I felt like it was time to break the curse and put my life on a different path. I wanted something different for my life. I wanted to be known for my achievements; not for being the party animal, or the not so flattering "clown" parts of a class clown.

HER

The Moment I Knew!

At this time, I had committed to giving Billy his hour as he requested, which for some reason he understood it to mean something other than just one hour. It had morphed into an hour every day. He was on this quest to win me over one hour at a time. For me, the question became what would Billy do with his one hour today? I was excited about the hour, which he had insisted on having every day. One Saturday evening, he asked me what I had planned on Sunday. I told him the only thing I ever have planned on Sundays is going to church. I told him I do not miss church for any reason. That's when he said he would absolutely love to visit my church with me. My first reaction was to say no because going to church is personal to me. It is my own private, personal time that I spend in worship to God. But then the guilt set in and I couldn't rationalize denying someone the opportunity to go to church, so I said, "Sure." During this time, I had been working out in the gym three to four times a week. My sciatic nerve started flaring up intensely. I did not mention it to Billy because I did not want to bring attention to myself. I wondered if he would tell by my slow movements. When he arrived at the house to pick me up for church, I was in so much pain, but I was determined to not let it keep me from church. I was still walking with noticeable nerve pain. While we were at service, I could tell he was intently watching my every move. As soon as service was out, instead of going home, he made a beeline directly to the emergency room. All of the incidences that ensued following this event were nothing less than eye-opening and amazing.

After church, I headed to his van thinking I could not wait to get to the house and get comfortable. Instead, Billy headed directly to the Emergency Room to get my back checked out. As expected, we spent the entire afternoon and evening at the hospital. Being the server he is, he never left my side. He was handling everything with doctors, the x-rays, requesting pain meds. He did it all and I was truly amazed. When I was discharged from the hospital, he gathered my belongings and took me home. He was the perfect gentleman. He was so caring and attentive. He helped take off my clothes and he helped me get in bed. He made my room and the house so comfortable. All I had to do was relax and get better. Everything was laid out nice and neatly within arm's reach on my nightstand. I had around the clock monitoring with my medication, eating, and the like. Michael, my son, called me when he heard I had gone to the hospital. He was on his way to the house to see me. I told him that I was not home alone. Mr. William is here taking great care of me. He said he wanted to come anyway to see me. Billy suggested I ask Michael to pick up my prescription that we dropped off on the way home. When Michael came into the house, Billy was in the kitchen preparing meals, washing dishes, and even loading the washer with my clothes. Michael saw that he was handling things and I did not have to. From my room, I overheard Billy thanking Michael passionately for picking up the prescription. He said, "This really, really helped me out!" This was the day I started looking at Billy differently. I remember seeing him walking down the hall and thinking wow, I had never been taken care of in my life! This felt so good. I was used to being the one to take care of everyone and everything. My eyes opened to the fact that I had this wonderful man taking care of me and I began to see possibilities in him that I simply refused to see before.

REFLECTIONS

Name something you've confessed over and over until it became a reality.

_____

_____

_____

_____

_____

Have you spoken something that may have brought laughter and doubt, only to have the confession come true? What was that seemingly impossible thing?

_____

_____

_____

_____

_____

Name a time you've experienced a paradigm shift that changed your initial thoughts or opinion about something or someone?

_____

_____

_____

_____

_____

_____

THE WORD IS OUT!

HIM

I Want the World to Know!

*F*or all of those who had been wondering about what was going on with us, they will now know that I finally found the one my soul loves. Billy and Darlene are together and are well on our way to building this relationship. It felt like I had been waiting to say those words forever. It was time to let the world know. Weeks ago, when we were in Savannah taking in all the beautiful sights and atmosphere, I had everything all mapped out. I knew once we posted anything showing us together on Facebook, curious minds would want to know. As things were picking up with our relationship, I was beginning to move into my role as Darlene's husband. A job that I wanted more than anything! We had a pretty smooth month and things were beginning to look positive as far as Darlene and I being on the same page with things. One morning, I woke up early and as I had been doing more often, I checked Facebook. I decided to post "Guess what everybody? I am coming home, and I am bringing home the trophy." I posted a picture of us sitting on the couch watching television. I intentionally selected a picture that looked like we were close and intimate, but we were just sitting on the sofa in the living room watching a movie with a throw blanket. Facebook exploded that day. I remember the look on Darlene's face after she saw the post. She looked so frightened. When her phone began ringing off the hook, she was afraid to answer it. Friends started calling each other saying there was no way the picture was what it looked like. They thought maybe we were at an event. The picture created so much commotion and a variety of comments, at one point, Darlene asked me to delete it. I was opposed to taking it down because at this point, the word had to get out. I could not wait to tell the world who I was with. I felt as if I had hit the lottery! This was a good time to show the naysayers that my intentions were not to take her down and ruin her life. My intentions were pure, and I was ready to show it to those who were still judging me based on things that I had done in the past.

My transformation started even before we got together. By this time, I was focused. I felt right with God and right with myself and my decisions. I like to say that this was the beginning of my journey to Darlene. It was also a shock for a couple of people from my group of friends. Going to the events together was a great idea because we could confirm everyone's suspicion at the same time. My friends called but they were not initially as direct in asking questions. Before that post, there were no pictures of us together but by now our friends were curiously trying to figure things out. They could not believe that I did not know Darlene from school. All of my friends knew her. That's the crazy thing about this whole thing. We went to school together. I was the class clown and she was the class president of the following grade; those are some of the most popular people in school. We both never missed a game or the pep rallies. The guys in the club we started were the "cheerleaders" at the girls' basketball game. Although UFG was all guys, that was our little twist, and we were at every game. If anything was going on as far as sports, I would show up as the mascot. Darlene and I had to have been in each other's circle, yet God turned a blind eye.

Now the saga begins. Things did not go over well with everyone. Her friend Frannie was the first to come out with a negative response and stopped talking to Darlene for months. Her first reaction was "I know you are not going to be with Billy. This relationship could not be serious." She didn't know what this was and did not want to hear about it. It was a little disappointing to have some of our friends feel as if we were just playing around. They said we must be joking. The momentum of everything picked up with speed since that day in Savannah on the beach. This period in our relationship reminds me of the scripture where it says that God will use foolish things to confound those who are "wise." To all the people who thought they were wise and thought they knew how our lives should go, God used something that may have seemed foolish and incomprehensible to confound them. He was like, I am God, you are not, and I know what I am doing. It was settled.

HER

*True Love Is Not Intended
to Be Contained*

*E*ven though I knew the sincerity of his profession of love to me, I could not shake the thoughts that it was crazy that so many felt that he did not measure up to what was best for me. I considered this time as being my 'watch and wait period.' To me, William Byrd is this happy-go-lucky guy who loves life. This man showed me discipline and focused commitment that I have never seen in a man. It was incredible to witness. I thought to myself that, by November 1st, if everything is still going well without any red flags, I could see myself going public with the relationship. Some close friends were on board immediately, and some were not. But knowing how they feel about me, I was not shocked. Frannie thinks the world of me. In her eyes, I always had mature, calculated, well-thought-out responses to life. She is very protective of me. She loves to talk with me regarding spiritual things. When she needs coaching, professional advice, or just someone to talk to, she would run things by me as a trusted advisor. Some friends and family members felt the difference between the two of us was too stark. The Billy they knew was smoking and drinking and doing things that I did not do. Occasionally, friends would make something for me, likely a spritz or some other sweet drink, but I was a novice. They said, "Darlene, you are incredibly involved in church ministry every Sunday. You are straight-laced. What would you be doing with Billy?" They were losing their cool. It was getting to be a mess. Imagine your daughter being with someone who you felt was a rebel. Would you say something about it? I'm sure they would ask. My children and friends alike were not having it. Some thought this was not a good idea. They were focusing on what they knew of Billy from his past. They could not see us as a couple. But those who were closer and knew both of our paths could see what God was doing way before I could.

My children believed that no one from Chester was going to have the mentality to be good enough for their mother. At the Christmas party, they saw us dancing together. Michael was there seeing us together at the party and watching Billy being loud and the life of the party as usual. Michelle commented that Billy makes mom happy, but they still weren't seeing me married to him. Although they saw me smiling and happy, they saw me marrying a pastor or businessman. I had to explain to them that that's what I am. That is not what I needed. What I need is what I don't have. I need somebody to bring into my life what I don't have and do the things for me that I can't do for myself. I need affection, friendship, laughter, and camaraderie. I said to them I am going to need somebody who is going to love the hell out of Darlene. Just because you are a pastor doesn't mean you are going to love the hell out of your wife. I didn't need a businessperson chasing after money or status; that doesn't excite me at all. I needed someone who will value me and love me deeply with words, time, and actions. I reminded my kids that I know how to hear from God. I assured them that I heard their concerns and was not love blind or lovesick. I will keep my eyes open and, if God says "RUN!", I will run fast. I promised my kids that. At the same time, I was asking God what He was saying. I am listening, what are you saying? I wasn't hearing anything. If you say run though, I am out. I was thinking: My kids - not having it. My friends - not having it. Even my cousin Kenny called me and said "Uhhhhh, what is this that I'm hearing that you are with The Byrd man?!" It was so unbelievable to every-body. I guess a lot of people were feeling like "this ain't going to work." Nobody could see us together. They thought this relationship would eventually blow over, or Darlene might be going through something. They thought maybe she's just cut-ting loose right now. Nobody was having anything to do with Darlene being with the "Byrd man."

The first stop was to meet up with my friend Kelly at a pool hall. She laid eyes on us and experienced our connection and interactions. As we were leaving she said, "I get it now!" She could see how we filled in the gaps in each other. The next stop was to Evette's house. When we sat on the sofa really close to each other, she looked at us deeply, then immedi-ately got Bernetta on the phone and said, "Let me explain to you exactly what I am looking at right now!" The next day, we went to the Thanksgiving party. Everyone was awaiting our arrival. Billy was immediately pulled aside to have the "talk." My girlfriends from the Bennett Homes Projects surrounded him like a flock of vultures. Zina, Debbie, Toot, Wanda, and Coochie were all gathered around him off to the side. They were literally plucking him and pulling his ears. They told him, "Don't you dare mess up on Darlene." They were smacking him around. They were pushing, pulling his ear, and hitting on him. Later, at another holiday party, before the brothers of the Class of 1983 (of which I was Class President) pulled me aside and surrounded me. Vinny, Ty, Louie, and others said to me, "Um...What's going on Dar?" I said, "I'm good, I promise you. I'm happy. It's all good." I was the protected one even growing up in the projects. They would say don't mess with that one. She's gonna be the one. There is something about her. I was protected and isolated. I wasn't allowed to go to many of the other neighborhoods even in my small city. It was good to feel the love and protection of those who only wanted the best for me!

REFLECTIONS

What are three things you are so proud of that you would literally shout from the rooftop?

_____

_____

_____

_____

_____

_____

What is something that you have been waiting forever to say?

_____

_____

_____

_____

_____

Describe a decision you made that might have been very unpopular, but you decided you would move forward anyway, despite naysayers?

_____

_____

_____

_____

_____

_____

TRANSITIONING
TO HUSBAND

HIM

*My Soul Has Found the
One It Loves*

*T*ransitioning to Darlene's husband is something that I had been dreaming about from the moment I laid eyes on her. What would it be like being her husband? Will I be able to make her happy? These were a few thoughts I constantly kept in my mind. Naturally, I was excited when we were finally at a place where God was beginning to transition the relationship into a solid foundation. I checked myself to make sure I was ready for the challenge. This allowed me to continue to be proven in my commitment and promises that I made from the beginning. I never made anything about me. Everything I did was all for Darlene. Yet, I still was not completely confident that she saw me as her husband, although we were both enjoying our moments together.

She once said, "Billy, you're nice to have around. I like how I feel when I'm with you." I could not stop smiling. Those words will remain with me forever. I did a lot of things to gain control of my actions. It was a discipline for me. I started doing a lot of things that I had not done before. I made them my habits. I wanted to change my old ways at this time. It was either, "go all the way" or "step out of the way." I could not afford to lose this great opportunity to have someone worthy of my love. I decided to step off that bus which was going nowhere fast and to begin to align my life with being Darlene's husband.

I started back going to church every week. I invited her to visit my church with me. She wanted to understand and witness my spiritual awakening and that meant a lot to me. We started attending my church together regularly.

I was learning more about Darlene and what she needed. I have never had a woman like her. In my mind, she was a spiritual giant. I would have to tell Darlene to stop being so discerning, but she could not because that is just how she is wired. She kept saying, "I won't do it anymore," but I knew she could not just stop. At the beginning of our relationship, it was very strange to me. The fact that she was consistently revealing things to me that I had not told anyone felt like witchcraft to me. Everyone cannot deal with her deep discernment because it weeds out things. She once told me that when she was at church, sometimes people would be walking toward her then suddenly turn around and go the other way. Most of the time, she did not have to say anything, but you just got a sense that she knew something. She said there is a lot of confirmation in that for her. If God tells her to say something, she is going to say it; but mostly, it's just a "knowing" that she gets on the inside. There is a lot of spiritual aware-ness within her. She sees under the covers those things that are not being said.

Darlene is unlike any other woman I have ever had the plea-sure of spending time with. I place her in a category all by her-self. In fact, this is my first relationship experiencing real, true love. I looked forward to proving to myself and others that I was capable of accomplishing anything I set my heart and mind to. I was focused on giving Darlene the best of every-thing she would ever experience. This relationship is different for me. Before I met Darlene, I was at a point where I thought to myself that I was ready to give up on women because I could not get it right. I cried out to the Lord and I made it a God-thing. I needed Him to help me! God, I am depend-ing on you to help me get this done, this is not something I can do in my own strength. This surrender to God was the real underlying part that determined if I would move forward with Darlene or give up on relationships altogether. I needed someone I could connect with. I was unable to connect with all the other women. They were either uneducated or not ambitious. There was always something missing, which kept me uncommitted. These major voids kept me from reaching my fullest potential as a man.

The changes were fast and immediate. When I am around my family, everybody smokes and drinks. These times were a test to show everyone the Billy they had never seen. When I showed up one year at our family reunion and walked in with a couple of cases of nonalcoholic beer, they had to chuckle.

That is all I drank that entire weekend. Darlene later told me that my family members pulled her aside and gave her "her props" for my transformation. Darlene later revealed to me that we were being looked at as if we were a Bobby Brown and Whitney Houston Story! She was a sweet hometown girl and I was the rebel.

Another thing that I learned about Darlene very early on is that she has a great love for her children, which I admire. I knew that I would have to present myself in a way to let them understand that the love I have for their mom is genuine and I will take exceptional care of her. The thing that I did not consider is that it would be quite a process to get them to feel comfortable with the idea of their mother with a new husband. There were deep discussions between her and her children about us. They staged an intervention when they learned of our engagement. I had never seen anything like it. Her three children flew in from all over the world. I was not a part of those discussions but I could tell that they were very intense and the children were expressive about their love for their mom, the values she instilled in them, and the bar that she set extremely high for them and lived it by example. They were not having it! They always remained respectful toward me. They did not hesitate to let anyone know that they were protective of their mother. That only showed me that they were raised well, with tremendous love and concern for their mom.

HER

*Observing this Undeniable
Transformation*

illy was transforming right before my eyes. I never told him to stop doing anything. In fact, I said if you want to keep on doing the things that you do, go right ahead. I had trained everybody and I was not going to train anyone else. I didn't want to be anyone's mommy. I was not going to try to be anybody's Holy Spirit. All I could do was be ultra-clear about what I would and would not permit in my life. That's it!

Billy never felt like a project for me. I've always believed that you can't put something in a man that is not already in there. All you can do is create the environment to bring forth what may be lying dormant. What I saw during our one-hour time is that he could be faithful, and he could be trusted. He was highly intelligent, even nerdy at times. We had great conversations. I was able to see his heart. He was a servant, not looking to be served, or taken care of. His work ethic was bar-none! I saw all the good things that perhaps other people never saw in him. Being as perceptive as I am, it is not possible to win any favor with me by telling me one thing and behaving in another way. I will hear your words, but for me, your words must match your actions. I must inspect the fruit! I had a chance to see a responsible man making the plans, making the phone calls, and paying the way. I saw him keeping his word. I saw an ever positive, friendly, spontaneous, and protective man. I saw a listener who filed away what he heard and acted on it. I saw an energetic, helpful, and thoughtful man – who was also kinda cute! These are all the things that I witnessed and these are the things that I love about Billy. Oops did I say "LOVE?!"

Reflections

When have you ever been blessed in such a way that it caused you to completely turn your life around (Blessed into repentance)?

Have you hung onto someone and loved them into their change with guidance? Who was that person?

What powerful things have you seen LOVE do?

THE PROPOSAL

HIM

*Be All Mine in Exchange
for All of Me*

The only person who knew that I was going to ask Darlene to marry me was my brother Darrell. There is no other greater friend outside of God and Darlene than my brother. I grew up very close to my brother. We are a year apart in age. We did everything together. We were never separated from each other as young boys. We traveled together as a unit. When we left the house, we left the house together. That's how our lives were.

A friend who was getting engaged asked Darlene to go ring shopping with him over several days. I would always ask Darlene how it went. One day, Darlene said she noticed this ring that captured her heart. It was a heart-shaped diamond and she said it was the most beautiful ring she had ever seen. It was a very simple band with a single heart-shaped diamond solitaire. She said it was very sweet, and the fact that the actual diamond was in the shape of a heart was very rare, but that the friend wanted a big ring with a bunch of diamonds even in the band. I immediately went out searching for a heart-shaped diamond. It was really hard to find one. I learned that they are rare because when you try to cut the cleft, they usually chip. That's why you don't see very many of them. The diamond can't stand the drill at that point where the cleft is and they usually end up as pear-shaped diamonds or something else. I found one and I purchased it.

Christmas was near and I was working hard at an onsite hotel project. Darlene absolutely loves Christmas and decorating, and this time of the season is major for her. Knowing this, I begin putting my plans in motion. I came over on Christmas Eve and found her fixing things under the tree. Christmas music was on, and everything felt festive. It was not quite midnight; it was maybe ten minutes to go before the clock struck twelve. I had it all planned out to happen on Christmas day, but waiting another 10 minutes felt like hours. Instead of waiting another minute, as Darlene was laying in my arms on the sofa, I gave her two Christmas gifts in one large box. In actuality, it was a box full of smaller boxes that were stacked like dolls. Each box was smaller than the one on top. Yet, each box contained a message with a special meaning to describe the gift. I could barely contain myself when she finally reached the last, smallest box. Within the smallest box was the heart-shaped diamond engagement ring. Her eyes lit up brighter than the lights on the Christmas tree. It was a moment of a lifetime and we both were well pleased. I said "Darlene, I love you with all my heart. I could love you for the rest of your life. You need a husband and I want to be the one. Would you please do me the honor of allowing me to be your husband?" **She said yes.**

Wait! Did she REALLY just say yes?! Honestly, I was so excited but still somewhat surprised. I was also now filled with even more determination. At that very moment, I had been called to a higher place with greater responsibility than ever before. I was called to be Darlene's husband. This was no small endeavor.

If you know Darlene and her Human Resources Consulting background, then you know she rattled off the non-negotiable competencies and qualifications for the job of "Darlene's Husband." But I knew she was who I wanted and I wanted to be her husband. I have never wanted any job in my life more than THIS job of being Darlene's husband. I have a huge learning curve - but I am up for the challenge. I am on autopilot now!

HER

Listening for the Voice of God

He gave me his heart, and I took it. Now we are engaged to be one. He promised we would honeymoon for the rest of our lives. He promised me a lifetime of vacations. He said he would always keep a pulse on our relationship and at least twice a year we were going somewhere to re-energize our marriage, which he felt would be so important to the honeymoon forever promise.

Now it is time to plan for the wedding. I had just paid for my daughter's December wedding, and here we are two weeks later talking about how we would put together another wedding. He said the best day in the world would be to get married on his birthday which is May 28th. We looked at the calendar and decided that Memorial Day weekend would be easier to pull off for our out of town friends. The date was set for May 24th, which was a Sunday during the Memorial Day Holiday Weekend. We started making calls and everything fell right in place just like that. It was too easy. Surprisingly, we got the venue with just 5 months out. This was the weekend of the annual jazz festival in Atlanta at Piedmont Park, and our wedding would be right in the middle of it inside the Park Tavern. Piedmont Park was also special for us because it was our meeting place for the Inaugural Diner En Blanc Atlanta. The very first time that I asked HIM for a date, I took him to this event. I asked him to go to a very special affair with me. He was so excited because I asked him to go on a date, and this event was a big deal.

Even with all of my preconceived notions as well as my apprehension, I knew saying yes to Billy meant that I would possibly experience everything my heart desired in marriage. I said yes because Billy was willing to take full responsibility for keeping a pulse on the relationship and for keeping his promises. His consistency and focus had been proven every time we spent time together. He was willing to be the man and take the lead. What I loved most about him is that I could trust him with my life. Our love is real, powerful, and undeniable.

As soon as we decided that we would get married and the wedding date would be set not too far off, we knew the emotions that would be invoked. This is not to say that we disregarded the feelings of our family and friends; the exact opposite is true. But when you have a solid relationship and can hear from God on your own, it is all you need to go against the tide of strong opposite opinions. Everything about our meeting and falling in love with each other has been extraordinary. Our only regret is that we did not find each other until now. We were made for each other, to bring out the very best in each other.

To our surprise, my children weighed in on the relationship and felt like we should pause and slow things down. Respecting their opinions, we decided that we would hear them out and give them an opportunity to express their feelings because we knew their feelings were real, but at the same time, they could not witness what the Lord was doing in bringing us together.

The engagement and the wedding all were happening extremely fast. I understood why they felt everything was rushed. It all made their head spin at the speed from the first meeting to engagement to getting married all within a year. We patiently allowed them to express their feelings and we were eager to bring them along on our journey of love when they were ready. But at this point, my children were not happy about the marriage. They tried everything to stop it from happening. They were calling my friends to ask them if they were going to allow this to happen. They asked me to come to the airport without Billy to meet with them. They said they wanted to talk to me alone to have some time with their mom. When I got there, it was immediately obvious that this was an intervention meeting to get me to reconsider the wedding. I heard them out, but in the end, I had to let them know that I am not asking for their permission to marry; but promised to consider everything they said and promised to run if God said to run!

They were not seeing the marriage. One of my sisters called me one night and I must say the call was bizarre. I held the phone to listen to what she was saying. I did not know what to say so I just sat and listened. My sister was in line with my children. When she first met Billy, she didn't like that he was drinking and was too loud. She and the children felt he was not my husband.

My whole life until this point had been all about my children. Once I became a mom, I took it for the team. I was not getting anything out of my marriage to their dad so staying together was not in the best interest of either of us. From the time my children were born, they were used to being mom's priority. I had made them my life despite my emptiness. At one point, my oldest daughter felt like they were being selfish not to understand that this was a time for mommy to be happy for herself. She confessed that I seemed so happy, so to think that they were not sharing in my happiness felt selfish. Everything was about giving my kids the best life. The move to Atlanta was about giving my kids a better life. Staying with their dad was about giving them the best life. They were given an opportunity for a better education than I had. It has always been all about them. I set the bar higher for them because of my experiences and what I had to deal with growing up. I even told them you should not marry anyone who is not on your level. For example, if you got a college degree, you should not marry someone without a college degree. If you have social standards or spiritual practices, your partner should have similar or higher standards. Because they were raised with this conviction, they felt that they were taught one thing, and by marrying Billy it appeared that I was doing the opposite of what I required of them. They felt nobody from Chester would be good enough for their mom; that the mentality would be off. They felt Billy was not stable and accomplished enough and therefore unmatched to marry their mom. They had a certain idea of the type of man they wanted me to marry. I understood where they were coming from, so I allowed them to express their feelings.

At the end of the day, this decision would be mine. Prayerfully, they will come to see the blessing Billy would be for their mom.

Reflections

What was the last thing that got your full commitment?

Describe a time when you honestly expected a NO but instead got a YES?

When have you intently looked for a sign or listened for the voice of God for decision direction?

THE WEDDING PARTY

HIM

This is Really Happening!

A wedding day confirmation came early on the morning of our special day. A Sunday evening wedding was planned, so I had every intention of attending service that morning to pray and set the tone for our day. Ronald and Annezette arrived the night before to stay with me and they agreed to attend church with me. As we walked into the church, we could hear that praise and worship had already started. (At this point we were worshipping in a movie theatre.) As I turned the corner into the room, the praise and worship leader stopped in the middle of what she was saying/singing and pointed to me. She asked, "Where is the lady that I usually see you with?" At this moment, I feel like I am on stage, everyone is now focused on me! I explained that, actually, today is our wedding day, and that my fiancé is already downtown at the hotel with her friends. Then she says this, "Tell her that God told me to tell her that she should go ahead and do what she was planning to do and that it is ok." Whoa,

I am overjoyed at this confirmation! It gave me so much confidence! I held my head high as I sat through the sunroof screaming, "I'm getting married!" while riding slowly through the traffic jam at Piedmont Park headed for my wedding.

Another memorable wedding moment for me was when my groomsmen and I were waiting at the altar for the wedding to begin. The hostesses had everyone assembled in the hallway. It was almost a half-hour off from the time the wedding should have started. Everybody was wondering what was going on. Pastor Nichols, the Officiate, said to us as we were all standing at the altar that he would go in the back to find out what was the holdup. By this time, I started getting nervous. I had all my boys lined up waiting in front of the altar wondering what was going on. They were not telling us anything, so we had no idea what was going on. The wedding is now 30 minutes late and my boys and I were the only ones at the altar.

The Pastor returned to the altar with a somber look on his face. He looked me in the eyes and said, "she doesn't want to marry you." The life was sucked completely out of me that very moment until he slightly smiled at me and said, "Sike." Pastor Nichols knows me well enough to know that was not something I would want to hear, but he also knows me well enough to know that he could get away with joking with me. When he said those words, it almost deflated me. He explained that the videographer was running late, and Darlene wanted the "Procession of the Wedding Party" recorded. I will never forget that moment. I later revealed to Darlene that it was not until I saw her walk down the aisle that I was sure that she would be my wife.

After the 2-step entrance of the wedding party, the music slowed to "When We Get Married" (Larry Graham, 1980). Darlene's closest friends came down the aisle, I knew it wouldn't be long now.

After this, Darlene would walk down the aisle to the song I picked for her to walk in to, "I'm Latching On To You" (The acoustic version by Sam Smith, 2012).

In all honesty, when I first saw Darlene, there was a big sigh of relief - things were about to go down. I'm about to get married to Darlene! I'm rubbing my hands in anticipation.

We planned to meet in the center of the aisle, and I would escort her to the altar. But as I approached her, I was overcome with emotions. When I reached her, I fell to my knees and began to pray. I acted on what I was feeling in my spirit and I needed a moment to thank the Lord for this wonderful gift and this very special occasion. After a moment of prayer on my knees, I stood up, smiled at her, took her arm, and walked her to the altar.

When the Officiate asked who gives this Bride, everybody in the wedding party stood up and said we do. That sound was so loud it sounded like thunder. Everybody read aloud the blessings over our marriage found in Deuteronomy 28. Picture time included a big giant selfie with 150 people behind us. The entire wedding party. Everything went off great and it was beautiful. We all had a blast. Our wedding day was perfect. It was the best day we could ever have asked for.

HER

They Said "Yes"

*O*ur wedding day was incredibly special. All our friends came to town and wanted to participate in the wedding. Most of our friends are like family, so we decided that our wedding would be a family and friends affair with grown folks only. We decided to get married in Piedmont Park for several reasons. The fact that the wedding would be on the same weekend as the Jazz Festival sealed the deal. The park is beautiful and during this time we knew it would be celebratory. We wanted it to be a special experience for everyone who attended. When we told everybody about the wedding, just as we expected, everyone had a similar reaction. They said they would not miss it for the world. My first thought was how are all these people going to be in our wedding. Everybody wanted to be in this wedding. Billy has tons of cousins and a million friends, without counting my friends and family. We kept going back to the mission of our union, which made it difficult to justify turning any of them away if they were willing to travel to be a part of our special day. It was an honor that they were interested in taking part in our special day.

Our wedding party included everyone who traveled to witness our love. There were 150 people, and at least 130 were from Chester. It was awesome to see everyone come together to celebrate our love. We told everybody about our wedding theme, the location, and the color coordination. Everyone was to wear the colors yellow, khaki tan, and white. Yellow was an easy selection because both of us picked it at the same time on the count of three! All attending the wedding had to wear yellow because if you are coming, you will be a part of the wedding party. While waiting in the foyer, we looked out and saw all the yellow, the ladies all had sunflowers in their hair, and the guys all wore yellow sunflower boutonnieres. We were simply in awe to see everybody walk down the aisle gleefully adorned in their yellow. They walked down the aisle with everyone doing the two-step. All the girls went to one side and all the guys went to the other. The guys all marched down the aisle smiling looking so handsome. Each girl had a chance to dance down the aisle to the song, "Let's Get Married" (Jagged Edge, 2000). Everyone looked so happy to take part in the wedding. The turnout was unreal, especially since the majority attending were not from Atlanta but traveled from our hometown of Chester, PA.

After the vowel ceremony, we were all outside in yellow taking beautiful pictures on the lawn. We were not expecting to see any of my children at the wedding. So, when we saw my son running across the crowded field at the jazz festival, we were breathless. He ran over to me and dived on me with open arms. His eyes were bright red and I could tell he had been crying. The only thing he said was "I love you, mom." That almost broke me down because I knew that was his way of saying sorry. That was his way of breaking from his sisters and showing love and support for his mom. His sisters were not living in Atlanta, so they were not able to watch the progression and transition of the relationship. Michael got a chance to see consistency and love since he was close from the beginning. He is the type of son who could care less about what you say. He would just watch to see what you do. Michael saw Billy loving on me , and serving me. He also got a chance to see some of the ways he would make me smile. Even though in his head he might not have been able to make sense of it all because his sisters had his ears, he became torn. His sisters only came home once or twice a year so they did not see us together on the regular, so for the most part they knew very little of our relationship firsthand. They did not have as much time to witness our happiness.

Confirmation of our marriage mission came instantly! We received a call the next day from a stranger who said, "You guys don't know me, but I have to tell you what happened to me at your wedding yesterday!" Her story in her own words is below:

Carmen Ford-Scurry

As I attended the amazing celebration of your union on Sunday my heart was overwhelmed with hope, joy and an immeasurable amount of LOVE! I prayed for God to reveal Himself to me regarding my situation. Upon entering on Sunday, I was pleasantly greeted!! Into the night her name was called repeatedly. When called I would turn also! Yes, her name was Carmen, too... lol. Later to my surprise I was assigned a seat at the same table with her... Shortly after being seated she stated "you have such a peaceful spirit I can feel it..."

I replied, "that's because we share the same name!"

I really wanted to share my testimony with her but didn't... inside I knew I should first share it with the newly wedded couple who poured soooo much into my spirit within minutes of their wedding ceremony!! During the ceremony, I heard a sound as if someone lit a match! The Bride's beautiful smile remains with me even while sharing this with you!

I must also share the fact I never met the Bride or Groom prior to attending their wedding. I accompanied my fraternity Sister.

During the reception...

The welcome was read by another amazing stranger (Frannie). She read the mission statement written from the hearts of the Newly wedded couple:

The mission of their marriage is to "INSPIRE, ENCOURAGE and IGNITE... to the TRUE meaning of LOVE!"

Wow! At that point, my purpose for attending a stranger's wedding was finally understood! Yes, Yesssss! Those words spoke LIFE AGAIN into my relationship!

So, I send to William and the lovely Darlene my heartfelt THANK YOU again for showing me/us what Love looks like!

Note: Carmen and Jerome were married one year later almost to the day, and Darlene and William were proudly in attendance!

Reflections

When has the outpouring of support for a decision you made surprised you? When has the lack of support disappointed you?

_____

_____

_____

_____

_____

_____

_____

_____

In what ways has confirmation for a decision been revealed to you?

_____

_____

_____

_____

_____

_____

_____

_____

THE PROMISE

HIM

A Promise Is Forever—in
Devotion to Each Other

I made a promise to give Darlene my heart, along with all of my love. I watched for and made note of everything that I saw missing in her life. I promised to aim to fulfill every desire of her heart.

In keeping with these promises, every month there was a 4-question assessment. I asked her:

1. What do you need me to do more of?
2. What should I do less of?
3. What do I need to start doing?
4. What do I need to stop doing?

I want to make sure that everything that I do for her, hits the mark every single time. My goal was to ensure that she experienced victorious living and that I receive an A grade for being HER husband. This constant assessment became an intentional part of our relationship and how we relate to one another. It was a part of our promise of a "forever honeymoon."

As we were spending more time together, I was realizing that the things that Darlene never had and needed were the things that I could easily provide because that is inherently who I am and what I wanted to do for her anyway. It seemed to me like the easiest and most fulfilling job in the world. I remember when we had been married for about six months. I was working at an airport south of Atlanta and had quite a commute. I used my traveling time as my quiet time, and I talked to God a lot during my rides to and from work. It was just me and God during my alone time in my car. One day on my hour drive home, I was overcome with an anxiety attack. It was the worst I have ever had. I began to cry out to God asking what am I supposed to do God? "Now that you have given me this gift, I do not want to mess it up. What am I supposed to do now?" I was driving home and thinking about everything that I could do to keep Darlene happy. I was asking God to tell me something and I expected an answer. "What am I supposed to do?" I felt completely lost and helpless. All of a sudden, out of nowhere, I heard this calm voice vividly speak to me. This voice was not like an inward voice that we are all familiar with. This voice very distinctly said, "***You take care of Darlene, and I will take care of the rest.***" It hit me when I heard it and from that moment, this was my primary job and I would take it on gladly. Then suddenly as I was driving down the highway, I started laughing uncontrollably while crying tears of joy. One of the happiest laughs I ever had in my life. I was so happy, and I remember saying "Thank you, God! This is just what I wanted." This is the easiest job in the world. It makes me want to cry every time I think of that moment. It was beautiful.

There have been very significant confirmations from God on a lot of levels. Darlene used to say that if God told her to run, she would. When she tells this part of the story, she says she never heard God tell her to run. You know Darlene talks to God. As we all say, Darlene's picture is on God's refrigerator. I know her relationship with God. His impact and influence on her life are undeniable.

When I was learning about Darlene and the deficits she had experienced with relationships and marriage, I committed to supplying all of her needs. And quite simply put, the things she needs are the things that I desire to give. I made the connection with the one who was worthy enough to receive all of the love I have to pour out. Someone deserving of every ounce of love that I have in my heart. I am learning how to be a real and significant husband.

HER

Promises Produce Expectations

e're married now! It's been a whirlwind. It has been a life-changing year. Watching my husband reinforced my belief that a woman cannot change a man no matter how hard she tries. The man will change when he is required to, when he wants to, and when he respects the woman enough to unselfishly be what she needs him to be. Billy promised to be the husband that I needed and to keep a pulse on the relationship. He promised to listen to me, trusting that I had his best interest in mind. I, in turn, promised to do the same. My past marriage had lots of downs, relationally. Honestly, I struggled to see how God was getting glory out of my enduring over 25 years of downs. I was His daughter. Who would want that for their daughter? Who would sign up to partner with someone for a lonely life full of downs? I signed up for the ups only. No downs! Meaning, I am not naïve to think that we won't go through the things that are inherent in life, but that we will go through them together and we will not put each other through downs! We're on the same team, looking at the issues of life together and strategizing on how to keep the opposition out. We determined that nothing or no one would be more important than keeping the peace and purity of our union with each other and the grace of God on our marriage.

Billy promised to pay attention and to create a marriage that felt like a forever honeymoon. Billy made a lot of promises, which of course, created great expectations for me. I signed up for the ups!

REFLECTIONS

What promises have you made? What promises have you kept? What was the driving force behind you keeping your promises?

_____

_____

_____

_____

_____

_____

_____

_____

_____

_____

When have you raised expectations or risen to the expectations of others?

_____

_____

_____

_____

_____

_____

_____

_____

_____

_____

_____

SOLIDIFYING THE MISSION

HIM

*Above All Else, Love With
a Serving Heart*

When you find yourself in love, you will absolutely feel that person completes you and makes you the happiest when you are together. Once you find this person, never let them go! True love brings more meaning to your life as you pour everything you have into pleasing that person. What makes you happy is seeing them happy.

What I think came out of the anxiety attack that I experienced on my way home that day was both a mission and a promise. If I take care of Darlene, God will take care of everything else. I realize that not all husbands operate as if they are on a mission from God... they may not feel the assignment. But my mission from God is to take care of Darlene, and I keep that in perspective every day. As long as I do that, I can rest assured God will take care of everything else. That's a FAITH builder! As I continue to take care of her, God has done just as he said he would.

He is FAITHFUL! We have never been happier. I serve her with little gestures like making her coffee every day, checking on her to make sure she is good, and kissing her all the time just because. I got her. She does not have to worry about a thing. That is my charge. Not all husbands are on that mission. My hope one day is to put this to practical applications for men. I think this would be a great platform to engage men. Darlene always says God would use moments like this to confound the people who think they know. God uses the foolish things to confound the wise. Thus, shedding His "LIGHT."

Constant assessments solidified the mission of our marriage and our expectations for our marriage. It is important to us that we share a lot about our love and our mission to help others in their relationships. This is our mission. Our love will inspire and ignite passion for many. Our love will give people hope that you can find true love if you are willing to love. We have a vision and hope that our marriage will be unlike any love ever seen. That is the kind of love I have for Darlene. This was on my mind while standing there on the beach. She said she wanted her toes in the sand. It was a no-brainer to me that if she wanted it, she could have it. Everything we do is with intentionality. There is an expected end and always in the interest of making each other feel loved even "as far as the water goes across this world." (Isaiah 11:9). I will be open and honest for all the world to see. I talked to God every step of the way from the moment I believed Darlene was the one for me. I get speechless even thinking about it now. I was pouring my heart out to her on that beach. I meant every word I said. I knew this was right, and that it was the right moment.

HER

Outserve Each Other!

ove gives more than it takes. Pure and simple. God so loved the world, that He gave. If you love something, you are mindful of it. You study it. You look out for it. You listen to it. You anticipate its needs. Billy kept telling me that no one has ever taken care of him the way that I do. He shared that no one has cared about his interests, his health, his needs, or his wants the way that I have. Most women are natural givers and caretakers anyway, even from a deficit. But women are also responders. The more they are taken care of, the more they want to pour out. Serving begets serving!

This was true for my husband also and the next thing we realized was that we were competing with each other! Not so much as in a tit for tat, but we were intentionally engaged in serving the other. We were anticipating needs, wants and desires and doing things to let the other know that we were thinking about them. We serve each other in the little things such as bringing a cup of tea or a glass of water, picking up small gifts, leaving little notes, sending encouraging texts and prayers, and beating each other to the punch with dishes and laundry. We were planning little surprises for each other and doing anything to bring a smile.

Our out-serve one another competition is ongoing and keeps our marriage balanced and selfless. We esteem one another and genuinely take delight in the happiness of the other!

I've got him and he's got me , we've got it all covered!

REFLECTIONS

When can you say that you served selflessly with a clean heart and motive?

_____

_____

_____

_____

_____

_____

_____

_____

_____

_____

What missional assignments have you been given?

_____

_____

_____

_____

_____

_____

_____

_____

_____

_____

_____

Relationship Scripture Map

A Life Map details some of the significant experiences in life that make you who you are and build your perspective of the world. Scriptures can be used in a life map. We have listed the key scriptures that resonated with us through the various stages of our journey.

- Romans 12:1-2 - I beseech you therefore, brethren, by the mercies of God, that you present your bodies a living sacrifice, holy, acceptable to God, which is your reasonable service. And do not be conformed to this world, but be transformed by the renewing of your mind, that you may prove what is that good and acceptable and perfect will of God.

- Jeremiah 31:3 - The Lord has appeared of old to me, saying: "Yes, I have loved you with an everlasting love; Therefore, with lovingkindness I have drawn you.

- Philippians 2:3-4 - Let nothing be done through selfish ambition or conceit, but in lowliness of mind let each esteem others better than himself. Let each of you look out not only for his own interests, but also for the interests of others

- Proverbs 18:21 - The tongue has the power of life and death, and those who love it will eat its fruit.

- Ephesians 5:25 - Husbands, love your wives, just as Christ also loved the church and gave Himself for her

- Ephesians 5:24 - Therefore, just as the church is subject to Christ, so let the wives be to their own husbands in everything.

- John 15:16 - You did not choose me, but I chose you and appointed you so that you might go and bear fruit—fruit that will last—and so that whatever you ask in my name the Father will give you.

- 1 John 3:18 - My little children, let us not love in word or in tongue, but in deed and in truth.

- Hebrews 11:1 - Now faith is the substance of things hoped for, the evidence of things not seen.

- 1 Corinthians 1:27 - But God has chosen the foolish things of the world to put to shame the wise, and God has chosen the weak things of the world to put to shame the things which are mighty.

- Matthew 3:16 - The spirit of God descended like a dove.

- Isaiah 40:31 - They that wait upon the Lord shall renew their strength. They shall mount up on wings as an

Eagle. They shall run and not be weary, they shall walk and not faint.

- Psalm 139:13 - For you created my inmost being; you knit me together in my mother's womb.

- Deuteronomy 28 - In its entirety.

- Philippians 2:3 - Do nothing out of selfish ambition or vain conceit. Rather, in humility value others above yourselves

- Isaiah 11:9 - They will neither harm nor destroy on all my holy mountain, for the earth will be filled with the knowledge of the LORD as the waters cover the sea.

- Proverbs 18:22 - He who finds a wife finds a good thing. And obtained favor from the Lord.

- Genesis 9:7 - As for you, be fruitful, and increase in number; multiply on the earth, and increase upon it.

Testimonials
The Love-Byrds' Affect

Nancia Leath, PHD

I remember the day Darlene came to my house. She told me about her then marriage. She told me how she felt about not being loved and not being treated like a wife, and the extent of how he treated her and spoke different things to her that made her feel like she wasn't enough. At this time, I was only married a couple of years and she had been married for over 20 years. I remember feeling her intense pain and loneliness.

A few years later, I received an email from one of Darlene's daughter's letting me know that Darlene was getting married again. At that time, I wasn't aware that she was even divorced. Her daughter was very concerned and said she didn't like this new man for her mom! I've always looked up to Darlene and saw her as a person I really admired. With her daughter being so upset, I felt I needed to reach out because Darlene was a mentor, but also a friend. She spoke into my life but also allowed me to speak into her. I went to Facebook and found the man. I wondered, WHO is this man? As a licensed therapist specializing in addictions, I saw something in the past that was concerning so I called her and said let's meet for lunch. I also saw a very different Darlene! She was alive and very happy! She didn't stop smiling! At that point, I said as a friend I have your back and I will be there at the wedding. I was so excited about being there and more than saying I am going, I said I WANT to be there to show support! After meeting with Darlene face to face, I felt peace and prayed for God's blessing over their relationship!

I was praying and seeing her so happy, and her confidence exploded as she was enjoying living! Knowing who she is in God is most important!

I went to their house for a party for Darlene's goddaughter. Billy had heard of me but didn't know me. I watched him and he was serving and making sure everybody was taken care of. Although Darlene wasn't there (she was in the hospital due to a spider bite), it felt like Billy was the male version of Darlene! I saw his heart. He loves people and most of all he loves God! I **felt at peace.** I was able to call her and interacted with her on her page and I just thanked God for what the enemy thought he was destroying - God actually created something more beautiful for her. The Lord was able to give her what her heart desired! Knowing Darlene for 20 plus years, I am thankful God was able to blossom something beautiful for her and for him. He is blessed to have her, and she is blessed to have him.

Byron BJ Johnson, Celebrity Stylist

I remember when both Dar and Billy were born. I know their families. Darlene's father mentored me into barbering. I remember when they met in Atlanta. They didn't know each other, although both grew up in Chester, PA. The odds were against them at first, as they seemed to be on different journeys. I had separate conversations with each of them. But after connecting, they became INSEPARABLE! The relationship was genuine, so pure and undeniable. The chemistry was unreal!

Once I heard about them becoming one, there was no doubt about their union. Since being connected, I saw them both grow spiritually and as a couple. There is no reason in connecting if you cannot make each other better. One day, Darlene's son came to the shop for a haircut. He discussed his mom getting married and I could tell he was not feeling it. I told him to just look in his mom's face and see the joy that radiates when she talks about him. Look at the aura around her! Look outside of yourself and see your mom's happiness. If you don't do anything else, I better see you at that wedding. He showed up.

Once you see them together, you see the joy in their face. To me, I feel the love they have for each other is on divine purpose. It is admirable. I am happy for both of them. This love looks good on them. We have been close since the night they met. When he came to talk to me and share his desire for her, I said we are going to change that outfit! That wasn't the only thing he changed! He wanted Darlene! I love them very much. I have seen him grow! I have seen him glow! He is more focused on his career! He has become more of a believer! Darlene is much happier! I see it all over her. I have never seen her frown. She has only been smiling since they have been together. They enjoy each other and their love is admirable.

Carmen Vaughn

When I think about Dar's journey to the present, I absolutely love her and Billy's relationship. It couldn't be more perfect. They say good things come to those who wait, well this was a wait and a half! Darlene is amazing because being around her and her past relationship, it was easy for me to see that it was loveless. What was extraordinary is that you would never realize how loveless the relationship was because she was so full of love. Her home was the spot to go to. Anybody could come to the house and she made them feel like this was their second home and they were a part of her family. When you were there, because of the way she is and who she is, you would never know that she was in a relationship where she wasn't getting that kind of love for herself!

When she met Billy, it looked like they were just friends at first, then she began to light up, she seemed refreshed and was always smiling and laughing. His personality is the bomb. When my family met him, we instantly loved him. He fit all those things you would want in a friend. Their relationship evolved into wanting to be more than that. He was like a fresh drink of water. I loved that she was so happy. It was so different! They were spending lots of time together, she was filled with joy and happiness. It was almost like she was a totally different person. They were a team, Darlene and Billy. When we saw that, we were excited. When they decided to get together everything evolved. Everything changed, even down to everything in the house! It was all unicorns and rainbows. They went on many trips and did all the things she ever wanted to do, and I loved it. When she was getting married it was like she was getting married for the very first time!

Violetta Queen Ester Harper, Author

"I KNEW... WE KNEW"

I knew when I saw him cleaning up the house - I knew! I Knew! I just knew he'd be the man of the house. My husband (who is her Uncle Pro) and I looked at each other and said, "Do you see what I see? Do you know what I might know?"

I knew... We knew! When we saw him at the house. No man just steps in and cleans for a woman unless his heart is geared, made, and created for her. I knew when I saw him moving around and moving about. Greeting the guest, caring for everyone. Checking on Darlene and making sure she was good.

I knew! I knew! God had heard our prayers. I knew that God was here in the midst using Billy to support, love and just "BE" for Darlene. I knew! I knew! I just knew! High school friends. Watching the relationship, watching the past marriage. Just watching, watching, listening to my friend, and praying.

I just knew! When we saw that young man moving around on a mission. A mission to love Darlene Yvonne! I knew... We knew! Her Uncle Pro and I would lay back and pillow talk about this mystery man. We would be like, "YO! This is the one!" This is the one! This is what Darlene's been waiting for. This is what Darlene's been laboring for. This is what Darlene's been crying out for. This is what Darlene was losing her health for.

Darlene is the epitome of Isaiah 40:31-41, "They that wait on the Lord shall renew their strength, they shall mount up with wings as eagles. They shall run and not get weary. Walk and never faint." She did that! She did that and almost did faint and almost did lose her life. She did that! She waited on the Lord.

And we just knew! We knew that Billy was the one! We knew it! The one to give back to Darlene all that she gave to everyone in her life and those she didn't even know in her life. She just gave! Gave! Gave! Gave! Loved! Loved! Loved! Loved! Darlene loves people just like God loves her. AND BILLY. We knew when we saw that he too loved people and Darlene like God loves people and Darlene.

We knew We are so happy, thankful, and grateful. We are moved to tears when we think about where Darlene was, what she has been through, and where she is now.

That's why I created the title "LOVEBYRDS!" And I'm so glad they're flying high like love birds because that's who they are "LOVEBYRDS," right up there with the dove. Darlene's life transformation when Billy (her Boaz) came on the scene reminds us of Matthew 3:16 when Jesus was baptized, and the Spirit of God descended like a dove. The "LOVEBYRDS" are right there and their marriage ministry is encouraging and uplifting. It is hope for generations to come and this book of their lives will allow their "LOVE LEGACY" to live on even after they've descended to Heaven. My husband and I have been together since high school, not sweethearts, but together for "36" years and we are so blessed to know we have another couple who shares our values and can help us in the ministry of MARRIAGE and continue to strengthen one another so we can together display the essence of GOD'S LOVE!

I knew... We knew that Billy Byrd was the one. We are still ecstatic! Billy Byrd, your Uncle Pro and Aunt Vie genuinely thank you for being obedient and answering the call. Pushing men out the line and making them fall. Doing whatever you had to do to make sure our special niece got her promised life. As you daily love and cherish her as your GOD-GIVEN wife!

Darlene, we sleep at night knowing our niece is above and beyond alright. The "HAPPY HARPERS" love yall' so much! We enjoy watching your love! We are honored to be a part of this amazing adventure. GODSPEED! I knew... We knew!

Chris Mann, Professional Actor
My admiration for the LoveByrds... William, affectionately known to many as Bilal, is my best friend. We've been good friends from the day we met. If there was a party or social event, we were the life of the party whenever we showed up. I remember at a recent holiday event someone mentioned, "Wow! Chris Mann and Billy Byrd together in the same room again!" He's My Brother from another...

Darlene (my sister-in-law) I know from the neighborhood. I actually knew who Darlene was before Bilal and I met. I spent most of my early years and then high school years in Chester's Bennett Home Projects. I was there so much, at my Grandmother's, that most people still think that was my home (in retrospect it was). Darlene was one of those people who I remember as having a good nature about herself. She always had a pleasant smile and a respectful demeanor.

Through the years with all the ups and downs of living, like everyone, myself included, we all go through what would be best described as "growing pains." So I've witnessed my best friend going through some of his. But since Darlene and Bilal have been together, I've witnessed such a positive change in his life. He'd always been one of the brightest people I've known, but he now has an extra pep in his step and a glide in his stride. He and Darlene together truly complete one another. I'm guessing it's what is meant by the term, "Twin Flames." You see the love they have for each other and the inspiration they draw from one another. It's a joy to see these two enjoying lives together. They are the definition of Love Byrds.

Made in the USA
Columbia, SC
01 February 2021